THE PREHISTORY OF CHINA

The Natural History Press, publisher for The American Museum of Natural History, is a division of Doubleday & Company, Inc. Directed by a joint editorial board made up of members of the staffs of both the Museum and Doubleday, the Natural History Press publishes books in all branches of the life and earth sciences, including anthropology and astronomy. The Natural History Press has its editorial offices at Doubleday & Company, Inc., 277 Park Avenue, New York, New York 10017, and its business offices at 501 Franklin Avenue, Garden City, New York, New York 11530.

Judith M. Treistman received a B.A. in anthropology from Brooklyn College in 1955, an M.A. from Columbia University in 1958, and a Ph.D. from Columbia in 1966. She has done archeological field work in the United States and Formosa, and has done research on Chinese art collections at The American Museum of Natural History and at Columbia. The author of a number of articles and reviews on Oriental archeology, she has had extensive teaching experience, most recently at Cornell University in the departments of Anthropology and Asian Studies. Dr. Treistman is currently associate professor of anthropology at the City University of New York, Graduate Center.

THE PREHISTORY OF CHINA

An Archeological Exploration

Judith M. Treistman

Published for
The American Museum of Natural History
The Natural History Press
Doubleday & Company, Inc., Garden City, New York

Text drawings by Jeanyee Wong

Text maps by Jerry Kuhl

THE PREHISTORY OF CHINA was published simultaneously in hardbound and paperbound editions by Natural History Press.

ISBN: 0-385-04594-8, Trade
ISBN: 0-385-04667-7, Paperbound
Library of Congress Catalog Card Number 76-160877
Copyright © 1972 by Judith M. Treistman
All Rights Reserved
Printed in the United States of America

For Peter

Contents

THE PREHISTORY OF CHINA

An Archeological Exploration

"The morning mushroom does not
know what happens between the
beginning and the end of the month."

Chuang Tzu (*ca.* 290 B.C.)

Introduction

Most Chinese history books begin with a statement, sometimes a paragraph, sometimes a single sentence, referring to China's past: "the three thousand years of literate civilization" that have made her unique. With this token paid, they usually rush jet-age style through the grey-misted centuries and breathlessly arrive at the gate to pre-modern history, the T'ang dynasty (or, if they are true traditionalists, the Han). It is our plan to take a more leisurely trip through the preliterate and early literate ages, treating as thoughtfully as possible the vast period of time usually encapsulated by the historians.

Our excursion will take us from the prehistoric past of two million years ago, when the first man-like beings are known to have inhabited Asia into the earliest literate periods, recorded in dynastic histories as Shang (*ca.* 1750–1100 B.C.) and Chou (*ca.* 1100–221 B.C.). This is the span of antiquity, the period which encompasses the beginnings of civilization and the development of feudalism and which precedes the great epoch of medieval China.

One of the unfortunate consequences of collapsing the history of ancient China has been to disguise the vectors of change, to smooth the rough edges of social movement and interaction into an uncluttered developmental curve, and thus to overgeneralize what is considered "traditional" or "classical" society. The method of archeology, which focuses our attention on the cultural details of human behavior, is a powerful counter to this tendency. We will be far less concerned with diffusion than with artifacts as relics of human behavior, less with dynastic and cultural successions than with the interaction of man and his environment.

Archeology in China has travelled an interesting, if predictable, path. Until the 1920's, it suffered the same shortcomings as early Western archeology, being largely restricted to the haphazard, and often unscrupulous, collecting of ancient art and exotica. The few serious archeological endeavors, carried out by educated amateurs, geologists, paleontologists, and the remarkable Teilhard de Chardin, can be faulted on scientific grounds (i.e., excavation techniques and laboratory recordings), but more significantly they fail on a theoretical level. These pioneering investigators were almost all Europeans, functioning in the milieu of colonialism. In order to explain Asia's past, they frequently invoked the "great migrations" and grand-scale diffusions that were currently thought to be part of the European experience. In effect, the early migrationists' theories retarded comprehension of the "idea of prehistory" by uncritical reliance on literary (and legendary) evidence, and by failing to seek the explanation of local phenomena in terms of local conditions.

The exception to the Western tradition was created by the sinologists' involvement with historical texts and documents. These scholars, mostly Chinese, had already painted in the backdrop against which the first significant archeological evidence appeared: the dramatic discovery, in the 1930's, of the site of Anyang, a late Shang center known previously only in the dynastic writings. The sinological approach has invariably led to ethnocentrism, an overly self-conscious awareness of uniqueness. Archeology in Asia is "political," and has been used by scholars in the new nations as a means of documenting an indigenous past, independent of Western historical currents. This emphasis, particularly evident in the work of Chinese archeologists since 1949, has unfortunately denied them the use of comparative methods of arriving at inferences and interpretations concerning national "histories."

It will be our attempt in this essay to look at ancient China unhindered by these two constructs. In order to do this, there are certain presumptions which must be made explicit.

We will insist on looking at premodern China without borders, accepting Owen Lattimore's concept of frontiers—vast zones of transition and interaction between social units not properly described as Chinese. Interestingly, both the Chinese political administrator and the dynastic historian have always recognized the nature of shifting frontiers. They explicitly named the minority peoples (even today numbering several millions) and treated them in a "we-they" relationship, whether in terms of economic exploitation (tribute), marketing regulations, or militarily through programs of pacification and conquest. The imposition of Western constructs of "borders" has hindered our appreciation of the cultural realities of the past. Archeological method impresses us with the evidence of diversity, with the recognition that ancient China was, indeed, a cultural mosaic.

Archeology and History

At the beginning of an attempt to perceive and retrace the pathways of prehistory, we are confronted with a semantic inability to express multidimensional time.

The Chinese philosopher-scientists, working outside of the culturally imposed chronologies of Judeo-Christian tradition and of Darwinian evolution, have always manipulated many time-scales. For them, the interlocking solar-lunar calendar provided a functional continuum on which they reckoned cyclical time on an astronomical scale, while simultaneously the "mechanical clockwork of the heavens" ticked away the decades. Against cosmic cycles which were estimated in the millions of years, naturally occurring individual cycles stood out almost in relief and were easily identified. Because it was never necessary to fit these into a "Great Chain of Being," the philosopher-scientists recognized the nature of transformation:

> All species contain certain germs. These "germs," i.e., smallest imaginable particles, transform into lichen and then plants. On fertile soil the roots and leaves of the plants give rise to insects and birds. Ultimately there is produced the horse, which gives rise to man. Man again goes back into germs. All things come from the germs and return to the germs.
>
> *Chuang Tzu*

This conviction in radical transformation was set into a framework which also recognized adaptation to different environments:

> If a man sleeps in a damp place he gets lumbago and may die. But what about an eel? And living up a tree is frightening and tiring to the nerves. But what about a monkey?

Chinese philosophers were dependent members of the courts of noblemen; they could not openly refute the opinions and deeds of their absolute rulers, but developed methods of persuasion and argumentation that were analogical rather than formal. The way of knowing was through observation, therefore they used evidence and proofs that were basically historical. History became the queen of the sciences, "the incarnation of the Tao . . . a continuous process, ever renewed."

The threshold of "history," which retarded recognition of the idea of "prehistory" in Western science, was nonexistent in Chinese thought. China always had a past—made explicit through literature but alive in continuous tradition. Thus in China the boundary between prehistory and history has never been real, and the culture heroes of the legendary past are the creators of the future, the inventors, engineers, and technologists.

The early discoveries of prehistoric relics were fit into the continuum of technological progress. In fact, the detailed past became part of the living historico-political tradition. By the third century B.C. a sequence of the "Three Ages of Man" had been described, including the ages of stone, bronze, and iron. In Europe, the similar scheme proposed by Lucretius had to await rediscovery until the scientific enlightenment of the mid-nineteenth century. In contrast, the Three Ages of the Chinese philosophers never diminished in relevance, probably because Chinese historical civilization was formed in the experience of many cultures with widely different technological achievements. So it was that Confucius may have explained flint arrow points as belonging to the Su Shen people, who lived in the northeast, and Han Fei Tzu, living during the Warring States period (450–221 B.C.), described painted and incised pottery of the neolithic, assigning these antiquities to the past, according to the traditionally reckoned epics.

The great literary age which began about the fifth century B.C. was in part an extraordinary embodiment of this fusion of past and present. Strands of social activity—political, religious, and economic—were interwoven along the continuum of time. The many "classics" of the age, the *Shih Ching*, the *Shih Chi*, the *Yu Kung*, the grand history of Ssu Ma Ch'ien, the philosophy of the *Chuang Tzu*, although each of a different genre, and not strictly contemporaneous, express this unity. Thus it is not inappropriate that we refer to them from time to time for the light they shed on our archeological endeavor; they were meant to illuminate the past for contemporary eyes.

CHAPTER I

Paleolithic Beginnings

Before looking into the human past, it is necessary to impressionistically wash in the background of environmental setting. Curiously, while Western archeology waited for the discoveries of geology to establish a chronologically calibrated lens through which to view the past and developed acuity along with geology, historical geography in China seems to have had a somewhat later and independent origin. Thus it was only in the mid-twentieth century that the evidence of an Ice Age (the Pleistocene) superseded traditional historical chronology. Although many Chinese philosophers recognized temporally relative definitions of space, topographical clues were apparently not read to explicate the shifting space-time continuum. This lack, more than anything else, retarded the emergence of "scientific" archeology in China; however, it did not prevent the historical absorption of the past into the present.

The first million years of man's existence were like infancy. Maturation, or specialization, was an incredibly slow and uneven process of experimentation until the internalized contradictions of biological potential and cultural behavior were realized in the human condition. Essentially, the significant environment in which human biological change and adaptation took place was a cultural environment. The physical environment nurtured and protected; it was a limiting but not a creative force. Only after the emergence of Homo sapiens did the natural environment become "cultural," and this is adequately reflected by the rich artifactual paraphernalia with which Homo sapiens ventured out into his world. We will see how, with efficient and specialized tools (tools to skin and butcher animals, to make bolas and projectile points), and knowledge of how to control fire, man as we know him (Homo sapiens) began to domesticate space. By the end of the Pleistocene, about ten thousand years ago, he had reached terrestrial limits.

The idea of late-emerging Homo sapiens is crucial to our understanding of early man in Asia, for the first steps towards spatial domestication were extremely hesitant; against the violent Pleistocene with its changing climates and topography, they appear feeble and unresponsive.

Of the Pleistocene, or Ice Age, in Asia, we know few details, but the general nature of events can be extrapolated from data gathered in other parts of the world. Although the gross geographic characterization of north and south is significant, it is better to make climatological distinctions, such as the continental temperate zones, the tropical Pacific zones, and the arid regions.

During the Pleistocene huge ice-sheets formed several times in Europe, North America, North Asia, and South America, and in many of the world's mountain chains. The spread of continental ice was fundamentally a result of changing temperatures and redistribution of precipitation. In general, glacial advances were marked by the appearance of a cold, damp climate and then by cold, dry conditions over the ice itself. Tropical zones were cooler and received less precipitation than at present, while the extreme climatic zones may have been more humid. There was a maximum fall of about 8°–13° C in the temperate latitudes, and a drop in the snow line. In Asia, Western Siberia was heavily glaciated, while Eastern Siberia and Central Asia were virtually ice-free. Glacial and periglacial conditions occurred in China's mountainous regions. In the tropics the temperature dropped about 4° C, which would give the annual mean temperature at the equator as 23° C. Marine temperatures in the warmest parts of the oceans cannot have dropped below 20° C. In other words, there was little climatic effect on the flora and fauna of the tropical lowlands. In contrast, the desert areas of the world were greatly affected by the changing wind patterns and distribution of precipitation. Pluvial conditions of increased rainfall during the great glaciations are known from every present desert area.

During the major interglacial phases the climate was similar to or even 2–3° C warmer than at present. More important to floral and faunal distributions were the rhythmic fluctuations in sea level which corresponded to glacials and interglacials. It is estimated that during the last glaciation, sea levels were depressed by about ninety meters, and during interglacial phases were even higher than those of the present. Thus there were several periods during the Pleistocene when the islands and archipelagos of the Pacific were connected by "land bridges" to continental Asia.

Against the major tectonic and climatic events of the Pleistocene, a cyclical countertheme of aggradation and erosion quietly worked to reshape the topography of the land. Essentially depositional activity took place during glacial advances, and erosion characterized interglacial and interpluvial phases.

In China, these alternations began with the erosional period which preceded the Poyang glaciation and the two consequent substages of deposition. At the end of the Early Pleistocene, a major upheaval (Huangshui erosion) took place and set the stage for the Choukoutien sedimentation cycle, during which gravels and reddish clay were widely deposited and loess formations were built up in the middle

Huangho region. These activities probably occurred during the Ta Ku and Lu Shan glacial advances. Once again a major erosional interval (Chingshui erosion) marked the entrance of a new stage, the Late Pleistocene, and the subsequent accumulation of vast Malan loess deposits took place during the Ta Li glacial.

These major "blocks" of time are useful in building a geological chronology for measuring the emergence of the hominids and the archeologically discovered remains of his enterprise. The interesting thing is that the tempo of human "development" does not march in time with the geological clock. A single species of hominid, Homo erectus, endured the alternations of climatological environment without essential change, and had a spatial distribution which was incompatible with precise biological adaptation to differing ecologies. It was this very generalized aspect of the early hominids that fostered their survival.

The study of paleoanthropology has had its "splitters" and its "lumpers," those who make taxonomic judgments on the evidence of minute details of variation between fossils and those who tend to recognize uniformitarianism in the ongoing processes of evolution—that the enormous potential for variation which occurs within single populations of the present expresses the magnitude of such variation in the past. The latter group of scholars generally identify three or four basic groups of hominids, Homo africanus (australopithecus), Homo erectus, Homo sapiens neanderthalensis, and Homo sapiens sapiens. The criteria of taxonomy are not all recognizable in the fossils themselves; some must be inferred through comparison with other primates and by analogy with living human populations.

The genus Homo is best defined by Buettner-Janusch:

> *Homo*—A genus of the hominidae. The structure of the pelvic girdle and the legs are adapted to habitual erect posture and the bipedal gait. The forelimb is shorter than the hindlimb.

> The hand has a well-developed thumb which is fully opposable. The hand is capable of the power and the precision grip. The capacity to make tools is developed so sufficiently that tools are made to a plan communicated symbolically from one individual to another and from one generation to the next.

We will permit ourselves to look into the dimly lit past for the heartbeat of man, although we can see only fossil and archeological silhouettes.

A rather unfortunate byproduct of recent paleoanthropology has been the renascence of the "Garden of Eden" concept in popular literature, a Garden of Eden which in theory still embodies the idea of a moment of creation but which has been moved out of Southeast Asia and into East Africa. This is a far cry from the ancient Chinese temporal outlook and equally distant from the complexities of contemporary Western biology and genetics. We must remember that fossils representing fewer than twenty individuals have been found in East Asian Pleistocene horizons, and some of these are very fragmentary indeed—a tooth, a jawbone, a piece of skullcap.

The majority of these fossils are of the type we call Homo erectus, a species which was widespread throughout the Old World by the time of the second glaciation. However, it is entirely predictable that tropical and sub-tropical Asia was inhabited before this, and we are certain that this broad ecological zone hosted the rapidly differentiating primates (such as the dryopithecines) during the Miocene epoch. Climatic conditions in South and Southeast Asia during the first glacial and first interglacial were not particularly harsh; it is possible to think of a protohominid or hominid fauna thinly spread across this southern zone. The habitat was hospitable to creatures as yet without the dexterity and creativity necessary to modify their physical environment through technology.

Thus far these very early Pleistocene hominids cast only spectral shadows, but we do know they were there. Back in the 1930's and 1940's, in China and in Java, significant paleontological discoveries were made but were not then compared to fossils found elsewhere in the world. The "discoveries" included the giant teeth obtained in Hong Kong drugstores where they were waiting to be ground into potent *dragon bone* medicine. In 1957, the Chinese paleontologists Pei Wen-chung and Woo Ju-kang reported on three complete mandibles and over one thousand teeth of "Gigantopithecus blackii" found by peasants in a cave in Kwangsi, South China. Although Pei and Woo consider these to represent a giant anthropoid ape, morphologically close to the hominids, other investigators have noted the strong resemblance of the teeth to those of the African *Australopithecus robustus*. This suspicion is raised also by an examination of the *Meganthropus* fossils found in the Lower Pleistocene levels of Java. The cave-location of the Kwangsi sites indicates extraordinary selectivity of habitation—either by an atypical anthropoid or, indeed, a hominoid. Neither of these groups of fossils has yet been compared to "Homo habilis" of East Africa, but there is an impression of similarity which is reinforced by the appearance of Homo erectus in very early strata immediately succeeding the Lower Pleistocene, and by the discovery in Shansi province of giant quartzite flakes and small "scrapers" in unquestionable association with fauna of the first interglacial period.

The ephemeral and transitory impression one gets from these incredibly scarce remains is replaced by a feeling of greater substance when we examine the next—very much longer—period, the Middle Pleistocene.

It was during the second glaciation and the second pluvial, and in the interglacial-interpluvial stage before the third glaciation, that small groups of men appear as infinitesimal but tenacious specks on the faunal landscape. Although two or three probable stone artifacts were found in the gravels deposited at the site of Choukoutien during this glacial period, the earliest yet known of these early hominid groups lived in Central China, in what is today Shensi Province, in the foothills of the Tsinling Mountains. The fossils found in and around Lant'ien are classified as Homo erectus and resemble the earliest Homo erectus fossil from Java. The distribution of this fauna is not unusual if we recall that during the second glaciation and consequent lowering of sea level the island was part of the Asian mainland, comprising the southern Sunda shelf, Sumatra, Borneo, and the Malay Peninsula.

From the first interglacial to the beginning of the third glaciation (a period of no less than half a million years!) Homo erectus, men with skeletons like our own but with smaller brains and thicker skulls, larger teeth, and heavy bony ridges above the eyes, ranged over the Old World. Lant'ien man[1] was living during a period when the climate was mild and somewhat drier than at present. He shared the grassy slopes with deer and hyenas, wild horses, elephants and monkeys, tapirs and stegodons. Because we think Homo erectus was a carnivore, we can imagine that he used the stone tools that are found near his remains—roughly worked flakes and pebbles of quartzite—as implements to help him butcher the chance-caught game, the fledgling bird, or infant mammal. They were also helpful for grubbing in the earth for edible roots and perhaps making little "nests" for the long evening sleep.

Indeed, if it had not been for the extraordinary series of discoveries at the site of Choukoutien, near Peking in Northern China, Homo erectus would have remained unidentifiable; he would have blended into the background without our retrospective recognition.

In 1921 a Swedish geologist, J. G. Andersson, at the time reconnoitering for fossil vertebrate beds in the mountainous area west of Peking, recognized the exotic occurrence of

[1] The fossils are probably female.

quartz flakes in limestone formations. These flakes suggested to Andersson that human beings had been present during the time when the cave, actually a fissure in Oldovician limestone, was filling up with sediment. Eventually, two human-like teeth were discovered, and in 1927 Davidson Black boldly assigned them to a new hominid genus, which he called Sinanthropus. In the next ten years a massive campaign was mounted, excavations were carried to fifty meters' depth within the cave, and more than eight thousand cubic meters of sediment were brought out for examination. Not only was Black's judgment verified (Sinanthropus is now generally recognized as Homo erectus) but one of the most complete fossil and cultural episodes of the Middle Pleistocene was recorded. By 1939, when excavations were halted by the Japanese invasion, the fossil fragments of forty individuals, great quantities of stone artifacts, and innumerable mammalian bones had been recovered. The Homo erectus fossils, once disturbed by modern technology, were not destined to rest eternally in shiny museum cabinets, but were casualties of the war, possibly lost at sea by the U. S. Marines. Fortunately, a German scientist—Franz Weidenreich—also a refugee, intensively studied and described the fossils before they left Peking. In 1959 the site at Choukoutien was reopened and excavations are yielding new materials.

From all the fossils we can compose a fair mental image of Homo erectus. He was a rather short individual, averaging about five feet in stature, but he walked tall. His limbs were just as ours, giving him upright posture; his head was heavy but small, set into his trunk with powerful neck muscles. He was agile on his feet, but his hands probably were not capable of fine manipulation of materials. He did not live the "good life"; 40 per cent of the population died before attaining the age of fourteen. Homo erectus (Peking man, as he is often called) had a varied diet, which is probably the only reason he was able to survive two major glacial periods of cold dry weather and one intervening damp, warm period [illegible] biological change. Collecting edible leaves, nuts, a[illegible] (there are enormous quantities of hackberry seeds f[illegible] in the cave refuse), he also preyed on the mammals which inhabited the area. Of the animal bones found in the cave at Choukoutien, 70 per cent are those of deer, while the others are of antelopes, sheep, sabre-toothed tigers, horses, hyenas, and roebucks—primarily the fauna of the hills, and rhinoceros, camel, bear, and pigs, the fauna of the low-lying areas. Peking man had no hunting paraphernalia and did not spend much of his time in the chase. Making stone tools out of quartz pebbles was a relatively simple matter of knocking large flakes off the pebbles and then removing smaller chips from along the edges of the flake by striking it with a hammerstone. Not all flakes were retouched in this way; some were used just as they were taken off the core pebble. There are no clearly recognizable "styles," or recurring forms, of implements. This suggests that the people either lacked the manual-visual control necessary to reproduce a stylized prototype or in fact were unable to conceptualize the end product of their endeavor.

We may well question the humanness of Homo erectus; was he capable of sustained abstract thought, speech, and the verbal expression of emotions? The answer, perhaps, lies in the ashes of his hearth fires. The cave at Choukoutien contains quantities of charcoal, and some of the bones of the animals that were eaten by men were charred, as though the meat had been roasted. But these bits of information tell us much more about the humanizing process itself. Fire, once controlled, not only gave heat and illumination to the cave home of Peking man, but it gave him the first non-biological approach to his environment. Fire was the first "technique," the first mediator between man and the nature external to him. With fire, Homo erectus began to domesticate space; fire extended the food-producing potential of his immediate environment, making inedible foods such as seeds, roots, and meats edible and nutritious. In the tropical parts of the world, fire was probably the primary technique of Homo erectus, used to drive and trap animals and insects and to clear the dense forests for encampments. With fire, Homo erectus began to domesticate time, altering the rhythms of daily life, focusing his activities on cultural rather than biological clocks.

Around a hearth, the individuals who simultaneously occupy a defined space become welded more firmly into a social group which has traditional meaning and continuity. The social need for communication is great, and one can well imagine the simple recounting of daily experiences in this context—experiences of past actions which require symbolic representation for telling in the present.

Although additional finds of Lower Paleolithic artifacts have been reported from two or three places, none have been so located as to give us a clear picture of the life and activities of the men who made them. From the succeeding stage of the Pleistocene, the third interglacial, there are some hints of improved technical control over the materials out of which artifacts are fashioned, but nothing to indicate a major change in the life style of the people or in the distribution and density of populations. There are small concentrations of archeological sites in North China, primarily in Honan and Shansi, which show a continuation of the stone tools known in the earlier period but also exhibit a certain inventiveness not previously seen. New minerals are selected for tool manufacture, and there is some experimentation with these new substances. In addition to the heavy pebble and flake tools, there is much more retouching of flakes (some are carefully chipped to produce parallel sides) and preparation of the cores from which the flakes are struck. This preparation of raw materials is most interesting, for it indicates the presence of just those features that we looked for in vain in Homo erectus: the ability to conceptualize the end product of one's labor and the capability to transform an "idea" into material results.

There is a great deal of differentiation of tools according to usage, and there is more standardization of artifacts; thus in this transitional period our definition of man is realized. The fossil evidence substantiates these impressions: Homo erectus is no longer present in Asia (we cannot even attempt to speculate on his "end" or if, indeed, he ever ended), and all the humans from the third interglacial and slightly later are Homo sapiens. The earliest of these are of the neanderthaloid sub-species. Significantly, they appear widespread in China, not only in the north, but in Central China (Ch'ang yang in Hupei), in the south (Mapa in Kwangtung), in the southwest (Liuchiang in Kwangsi and Tzeyang in Szechwan). The last two fossils are rather securely dated to the Upper Pleistocene, the time of the fourth and last glaciation.

The awesome, pervasive homogeneity of the early Lower and Middle Paleolithic has been described; we have suggested that it was a function of the essential contradiction in hominid evolution, the contradiction between the biological and cultural modes of survival. The unity that we have seen in the Lower and Middle Paleolithic was largely a biological unity; the diversity that appears in the remains of Upper Paleolithic man is the product of varying cultural approaches to existing environments. The Upper Paleolithic, a product solely of Homo sapiens, everywhere gives testimony to the emergence of the uniquely human experience, the cultural manipulation of the quality of life. The conquest is the victory of technology, but it is the result of the efficient and economic organization of conceptual thought and social arrangement made possible through the use of complex language.

This is why the Upper Paleolithic, as it has been discovered in Europe, has always been called "brilliant," "dazzling," etc. Where is the Upper Paleolithic in Asia? We search almost in vain, and when we do perceive it, the splendor is not present. As yet, no cave paintings, no lovely carved figurines, no elaborate burials have been found. It is doubtful if the lack can be explained entirely by underexploration; it exists only if we try to cast the human component in the Late Pleistocene of Asia in a mold shaped to European configurations. If we accept the Upper Paleolithic as a biotechnological stage, a stage of humanization, of the cultural fragmentation or specialization of populations struggling to achieve realization through their confrontation with localized ecologies, then the scarce archeological remains in China witness this stage.

In restricted localities there are correspondences to the European Upper Paleolithic, and these are readily identifiable and instructive. Scattered over the present-day grasslands of the Ordos region (around the "big bend" of the Huang, including parts of Inner Mongolia, Ninghsia, and northern Shensi and Shansi provinces) are the exposed sites of prehistoric human occupation. These "buried" sites are hidden, except for rare instances of weathering or the downward cutting activity of streams, below tens of feet of loess and waterborne sands. About thirty thousand years ago, during the last glacial period of the Pleistocene, men camped on the open steppes. It was cold, and the dry, dust-laden wind swirled almost continuously. The people made tools out of flakes or quartzite, silicified limestone, and flint. Stone cores were carefully prepared in advance so that the largest possible number of flakes could be removed from each nodule and the sharp edges of the flakes would be fairly regular. This economy, or efficiency in the use of raw materials, is also reflected in the small size of the tools. At the site of Sjara-osso-gol, which may have been an oasis, with more abundant vegetation and game, they travelled long distances to bring back the black quartzite out of which they made their tools.

Some type of shelter was necessary for survival, and we can imagine small clusters of tents dotting the plains. Nothing remains to tell us about their dwellings, but the tools themselves are a component of the whole technology. They used the little scrapers, sometimes retouched at the terminal end or along the sides, and sometimes hafted in bone or antler, to treat animal skins, to scrape away the fat and flesh and soften the hides. Without this process the skins were useless —brittle and hard; with constant rubbing, the skins became soft, flexible, and durable. They could be fashioned into the tents and blankets that made living in the harsh climate bearable. The Ordos of thirty thousand years ago was not a wasteland: large herbivores wandered in great numbers over the open stretches of vegetation, and on these herbivores man subsisted. At Shui-tung-kuo, the charred and broken bones of bison and wild ass were strewn about the floors and around the hearths; to a lesser extent, the bones of wooly rhinoceros and hyenas, gazelles, antelopes, and ostriches were found. The rich artifactual and faunal debris at Sjara-osso-gol suggests that this was not a temporary encampment. The density of broken animal bones and other remains (including over three hundred gazelle horns!), the refuse pits filled with waste chips of stone and the bones of small rodents, birds, and bats indicate year-round occupation. Perhaps the diverse potentialities of the environment, the oasis bordering on the drier steppeland and on the forested southern fringe of the Ordos, permitted the people to make occasional forays abroad for deer, wolves and wild boars.

The people of the Ordos came close to being the "big-game hunters" of Asia, and in this they resemble the Pleistocene hunting groups of Europe and Siberia. However, this very special way of life, stimulated by a unique set of environmental circumstances, was only one of the varied cultural developments that took place during the Upper Paleolithic.

There is evidence of Upper Paleolithic occupation of other

areas of China, and these almost everywhere flow across the chronological boundary of the Pleistocene and into the so-called Recent period. The sociotechnological activities which characterized this long episode in cultural development are expressed in the specialization of stone-tool manufacturing processes, best seen in the southwestern hill country of Szechwan. Along the Tatu River in Hanyuan hsien, the remains of a hunting-gathering community were found in loess deposits of the very Late Pleistocene. Along with the charcoal of their cooking fires and the debris of their meals (mostly deer meat and shellfish) were the small flake tools, scrapers and knives, with which they worked. The preparation of stone cores and the occurrence of blades resemble the Ordos assemblages.

In present day Kweichow, in Yunnan, in Mongolia and Shantung, hints of human activity come through the archeological fog. Always lacking the explosive quality of the big game hunters, and probably living in very small populations, the Upper Paleolithic people were experimenting with a way of life which was not nomadic but which began to intensively explore the limits of local ecosystems.

Elsewhere in North China the stage is set for cultural events of the succeeding, post-Pleistocene period. We can get a glimpse of the transition itself at the site of Choukoutien, this time from the Upper Caves, which were frequented by man at the very end of the Ice Age and probably during the warmer phase immediately following. Five very thin layers of deposits within the cave contain the evidence of human occupation. Only twenty-five stone implements remain to tell the latter-day scientist of the daily activities that took place in and around the cave: in fact, the scarcity of tools suggests that the location was used only for temporary shelter and not permanent habitation. These few bits of stone are significant, however, because they represent the continuous practice of tool-making techniques first seen in the Lower and Middle Paleolithic. In addition to the pebble and flake tools, there are small scrapers. Technical experiments with new materials marked the period of transition—the working of bone and antler was added to the repertoire of skills. Awls and an eyed needle, drilled beads of limestone, sea shell, and the teeth of rodents and tigers proclaim the self-awareness of the men who wore clothing of leather and adorned themselves with the lustrous beads. For all time man had separated himself from the environment, from the natural world. The Upper Cave at Choukoutien was most probably a place of burial for a group of men who lived on the plains or perhaps on the shore of a nearby lake. Inside the cave were the fragmentary skeletons of seven people, a man of great age, a younger man, two young women, one adolescent, and two little children. We can know neither who they were nor how they died. But friends and relatives carefully interred them and scattered hematite—the red of life—all about.

In this ancient burial we have once again recognized man. In defiance of the natural world, Homo sapiens proclaimed the victory of cultural time over the biological clock. Perhaps the irony of the cultural conquest is best seen in the epilogue to this episode: the roof of the cave collapsed and crushed the skeletons buried beneath.

CHAPTER II

Technology and the Natural World

When the historian or the social scientist wishes to study human behavior—past or present—he asks questions. He asks questions of the documents written during contemporary times and of the people participating in current or past events. He is surrounded with words, words of description, words of explanation, confirmation, and contradiction. In all the noise manufactured by such inquiries he perceives the messages, and, applying the grammar of his discipline, he proceeds to reconstruct the events and processes —the content and structure—of behavior.

The study of human prehistory takes place in silence. When the archeologist unearths a flint tool, he cannot ask: How did you make the tool, what did you use it for, was it a good tool? He cannot ask, if it is an arrow point: What game were you hunting, how many did you kill, were you joyful? If the arrow point was found in a grave, lying alongside the deceased, he cannot hope to know who attended the funeral, what songs they sang, were they sad. And yet, embedded in the very nature of archeological remains, the message exists.

Prehistoric archeological remains tell us about the intersecting spheres of social behavior and environment, i.e., the technology of a group of people living in a bounded space at a given point in time. The prehistorian attempts to elicit data by directing his questions at this area. Awesome and imperfect, communication through the generations of silence is begun.

One possible kind of questioning assumes that one's perception and categorization of the environment is largely structured by technology. Of course, we cannot pursue this on an individual level, for it is not a physiological "fact," it belongs to cultures. A very simple example can be found in geography. Franz Boas, in a study of the geographical terminology of the Kwakiutl Indians of the Pacific Northwest, discussed the linguistic significance of the technology of subsistence. Instead of the familiar (to us) points of the compass, the Kwakiutl, a seafaring people, oriented themselves to the directions of the coastline and the rivers: "downriver," "down along the coast" = north and west, "upriver," "up along the coast" = south and east, "inland" = away from the sea or river, and "seaward" = away from the land. Geographical terms then refer to specific locations relative to these directions: "beach facing downriver" = westward, "region alongside inland," etc. The very numerous names for islands are locational, frequently being designations of a goal or journey. Thus a specific island may be named "the seeing of the beach." There are many names that incorporate information necessary for successful navigation: "place having swell inside," "receptacle of the northwest wind," etc. Other place names are descriptive of topographic features or natural characteristics: places "having sockeye salmon," "having blueberries," or places "for halibut fishing."

Another level of inquiry is the secondary recognition by archeologists of the microenvironments recognized and utilized by the early inhabitants of an area. We will attempt to do this for Asia, taking a "slice-of-time" approach which cuts through history and looks at the cultural map at a given point in time. The period is about 5000 to 2000 B.C. The picture is one of diversity, fulfilling our expectations (built on ethnographic evidence) that the technological-cultural configurations found in prehistoric Asia are remarkably close to the great geographic "blocks" of the topographic map. The persistence of this diversity into historical times is extraordinary, but understanding its ecological underpinnings makes us realize that "environment" has a shifting quality when viewed historically. Environments can be seen only in relation to the technology; i.e., added or changed technology redefines and restructures, recategorizes the "significant environment." As we travel through time, the ecological opportunities exploited by man have changed and are changing. Therefore, it is absolutely necessary to discard our vision of Asia of today—the great unity of an agriculturally dominant technology—and look backwards to the significant geography of the non-agricultural inhabitants.

If we follow the characterization of Asia's geography suggested by J. E. Spencer, and describe only the "bare landscape," then we can picture the arctic fringe of Asia as an extension of the European lowlands. The central and southern Siberian Plain is a broad zone of ancient rocks, folded and faulted many times in the past. The eroded roots of mountain ranges, plateaus, and massifs form a very rugged region which serves as headwater zone for many of the arctic-flowing rivers of Siberia. South of these are the great basins, Turkestan, the Tarim, Dzungaria, and the Mongolian plateau. The mountains are very high, the depressions deep.

Southward once again, and the great Tibetan plateau rises up; high enclosed basins set apart by mountain ranges running east–west. These are part of the Alpine chain that reaches across Eurasia. The eastern mainland of Asia is varied; units of mountains and flatlands crisscross each other in Eastern Siberia, Manchuria, and China. In the southern part of the mainland, recent depositional basins are sandwiched into the Tertiary Alpine chain which runs down the Burmo-Malaysian peninsula.

The Forest Efficiency

Man claimed this skeletal landscape and fashioned ways of life, styles of existence that waxed and waned, blended and, in the end, confronted one another. And here the heights of great civilizations were reached, sometimes incorporating and sometimes surrounded by the millions who lived the minor traditions of the uncivilized, the savage, the barbarian. Looking at 5000–2000 B.C. as a slice of time, there were two major modes of survival and adaptation, each destined to speciate and create new ways of utilizing the environment and thus creating new ecologies. Both early technologies signify a cultural response to the natural conditions of the post-Pleistocene, a response which involved the "anchoring" of populations in those favored regions in which it was possible to develop patterns of intensified collection of wild vegetal foods and the resources of rivers. Out of the economic foundations achieved by these sedentary populations grew a primary farming efficiency (familiar to us from Near Eastern prehistory) and, what has been called in the New World examples of non-nuclear development, the primary forest efficiency. Although we may argue that in Eastern Asia the agricultural innovation could have proceeded only from the primary forest efficiency, it is also true that it was an economic system from which many peoples did not depart until very much later.

The concept of "forest efficiency" is used in North America and in Europe to embrace and explain the successful exploitation of natural food resources which leads to and supports residential stability, accumulation of personal goods, frequently some degree of craft specialization, and a resistance to the introduction of agriculture. In ancient Eastern North America, the relation between man and environment was

Fig. 1 Map of East Asia

achieved by delicate adjustments in seasonal technology which exploited the natural abundance of the forests and rivers and of the bays and estuaries of the coast. Concentration of populations occurred where the natural community became specialized to a degree that made seasonal movement unnecessary: collection of shellfish, both fresh water and sea mollusks, and the collection of nuts (especially acorns) in the deciduous forest zone. The richness of life of these communities is mirrored in the differentiation of styles that mark the material productions of the various cultural regions that grew up and persisted until the European colonization.

By approaching Asia with this "non-nuclear" approach, it is possible to delineate at least ten cultural "regions" at about 5000–2000 B.C. Further archeological exploration, especially of mainland Southeast Asia and South China, will undoubtedly reveal more, just as this huge time block will be refined. It is best to first view these regions through a wide-angle lens and then gradually focus in on China itself.

EASTERN SIBERIA

Eastern Siberia is composed of many geographic subregions, but the highlands of the southern and central portions have a "unity" achieved through an extensive network of waterways and the unending taiga. Although the climate is harsh and has probably been so since the altithermal phase of early post-Pleistocene—the relatively open forest of larch and pine, birch, poplar, and aspen is abundantly populated with large grazing animals—the elk, reindeer, deer, and the brown bear. Lynx, squirrel, rabbit, beaver, and game birds such as the grouse are plentiful.

The mountains which stretch from Lake Baikal to the Amur River are high, sometimes reaching 11,500 feet, and the river valleys are broad. The modern-day visitor to Eastern Siberia is still overwhelmed by the forests—the little villages with houses built of logs and elaborately carved wooden façades have split-rail enclosures which bravely isolate the people from the forest and tie them to the national network of highways. But behind every village is the forest.

Six thousand years ago, bands of people wandered in small communities through these woods, settling temporarily for seasonal hunting activities. They no longer lived in semi-underground lodges but in light tents. The heritage of tool-making traditions—the small flakes and blades of the Paleolithic—was reshaped as composite implements and missiles were manufactured. Slotted knives with side-blades were used for butchering small animals and birds, the bow was reinforced by the addition of a bone backing and arrow points were carefully retouched and stemmed for hafting. The people made pottery, at first crudely fired and decorated only by the nets in which they were fashioned, but later the surfaces bore textured designs that resulted from the use of a paddle to thin the vessel walls. Many of the pots have pointed bottoms and were probably set into the earthen floors of the dwelling. The use of permanent containers suggests that the women may have been collecting the wild products of the forest—berries, nuts, and edible plants. A new stone tool tradition of large pebbles and flake scrapers, half-ground axes and adzes appears. These may have been used to clear away the forest in preparation for living sites, for digging storage pits, for stripping bark, for working skins to make them usable for garments and blankets and to chop wood for the much-needed fuel. Gradually as the people became comfortable in the forest there was a perceptible shift in the economy as the resources of the rivers were made available through a wide range of inventions. A complex and elaborate fishing technology developed, including barbed hooks and harpoons and even little stone fish "lures" which were probably drawn under the ice.

The more secure economic life is reflected in the construction of relatively permanent settlements, and in the cemeteries, where the bones are found stained with red ochre sprinkled during some ritual of death. The dead were almost always interred with the useful equipment of the living. Life itself was rich, as the villagers settled on the banks of the rivers and lakes that provided sustenance.

In time, the populations of the taiga came to know the agriculturists of the south but did not change the basic style of their lives. They continued to function in an environment most effectively and successfully shaped by their forest technology and did not attempt what would have been a doomed experiment with cultivation. The light podzolized soils of the taiga are acid, there is only a thin topsoil low in humus content, and it is underlain by an unproductive leached silica-bearing soil.

Eventually, metallurgy was introduced, and a native bronze industry was stimulated to smelt and cast ornaments and utilitarian objects such as needles and knives. They took much care with the making of their clothing; leather aprons were decorated with string upon string of shells and mother-of-pearl beads. Look at the people as they appear on a contemporary rock painting: a row of birch bark boats, the passengers seated with arms raised to the sky, and, supporting the whole, a doe surrounded by "men" dressed in costumes of the deer with antlers on their heads. The river, the animals they hunt, the forest to which they are bound.

In Chita Oblast, where the Amur River joins the Shilka River, a valley adaptation of the taiga way of life took place around 3000 B.C. In many ways it is similar to the culture of the Baikal, incorporating the now familiar details of technology but elaborating even further the exploitation of the rivers. In the northern reaches of the Amur, the unity of the taiga is broken by local ecological patterns. The coniferous forests of the north with the prevalent larch in the west and spruce in the east merge with the deciduous forest of the south, gradually becoming lost in the fantastic Manchurian flora: blue cedar, silver fir, maple, linden, oak, and birch. In the river valleys, there are over 150 species of trees including elm, ash, cork-oak, and the wild apple and pear. The watersheds are covered with a deep blanket of grass. In prehistoric and early historic times, people approached this environment with confidence, built of an efficient fishing and hunting technology. These were the "paleo-asiatics" of the ancient past, perhaps the ancestors of the great tribes of later millennia—the Tungus, the Manchus, and the Mongols.

Archeologists have discovered a prehistoric site in a cave on the Shilka River which tells us much about these people. The cave was used as a temporary dwelling place by small parties of hunters, although it has been suggested that it had been a burying ground for even earlier inhabitants of the valley. The cave was a "total" home, and we can imagine the men returning after the day's activities along the river where they fished with complex tackle and with apparent success—great heaps of fishbones were found in the caves. The diversity of fishhook types suggests that they knew the habits of many different species of fish: the bottom feeders, those which frequented the rocky banks and the dense weeds, etc. They speared and harpooned larger fish, used nets, and probably constructed weirs. A roll call of animals hunted emphasizes the natural abundance of the forest environment and the technology of man: wolf, polecat, mountain sheep, musk deer, roe deer, wild boar, elk, weasel, flying squirrel, fox, lynx, snow hare, mouse, rat, hamster, marmot, and sable. The trappers who made this region so attractive to European fur traders in the eighteenth and nineteenth centuries used techniques which must have been known to prehistoric man. The one domesticated animal was the dog, which was probably used for food and clothing but most significantly for transportation. In this latter capacity of draft animal, one which was important to later tribesmen as well, the dog was part of the technology of forest efficiency.

The technological aspect of this efficiency was substantially improved by the development of composite tools and weapons for hunting. Combinations of stone and bone gave the technician a greater range of solutions to functional problems in tool design and made possible more economical use of available raw materials. There were no specialists in tool production; the cave-home was a workshop as well, and scattered on the floor is the debris of preparation—the stone pebble "blanks," unretouched and broken lamellar blades, the partially cut bones, etc.

In the absence of agriculture, the women involved themselves with the forest by searching out and collecting wild fruits and vegetables; fibrous plants were gathered later to be worked with comb-like bone implements to manufacture string. In turn, the string was twisted into fabrics (textile impressions are found on the pottery) and probably nets. The pottery vessels themselves were quite large, and we can assume that they were used to store foods and water. Broken pots were carefully repaired by passing thongs or strings through holes drilled in the vessel walls. In addition to the impressions of the cord-wrapped paddle, many pots were "check stamped" and "ribbed" by pressing preshaped bone implements into the soft clay. The ornaments with which the people dressed themselves celebrated the forest—the perforated boar tusks, probably worn as necklaces, the strings of shell beads, and the small plaques of mother-of-pearl that were sewn onto their garments.

Somewhat later in time (about 2000 B.C.) and not yet clearly identified as to origins and cultural relationships, the people of Maritime Siberia had carried the technology of fishing even further. Large villages of one hundred or more households were supported by an intensive harvesting of the wild-life of the seashore and the rivers. In addition to hunting the deer, boar, and small animals of the forest (forests later destroyed by agricultural man and replaced by high grass steppelands), the people of the "shell mound cultures" knew well the habits of waterfowl and counted as fair game the mallard, bean-goose, gadwall, spoonbill, goldeneye, scaup, grebe, and the great cormorant! They caught the large-billed crow and pheasants and domesticated the chicken. They also kept pigs and dogs. But above all, they collected shellfish (over twenty-three species of mollusks have been identified) and crabs, and trapped the plentiful tuna that swam against the tides and found themselves stranded in bays and estuaries. In the Maritime province as in the Amur region, the people were in contact with the Chinese agriculturalists but did not change their way of life until the introduction of iron indeed changed their environment. The Chinese chronicles speak of the Tungus, the Goldi, the "fish-skinned" people; the eighteenth-century Russian explorers describe their clothing made of fishskins laboriously softened and sewn into garments "even socks and boots."

THE TUNGPEI

As the Amur River cuts eastward from the Shilka Valley, it defines the northern boundary of the Tungpei, the huge territory known mistakenly in English as Manchuria. The central area of Tungpei is the great Manchurian Plain surrounded by a mountain system cut by three major rivers, the Nonni, the Sungari, and the Liao. The plain opens only in the south towards Liaoning. It is a geographically isolated region, at present characterized as typical steppeland in which wild oats, wormwood, and feather-grass prevail. There are many salt lakes and marshes and occasional shifting sand dunes. Forests are supported only along river banks. Over a period of many years archeologists have slowly uncovered the remains of prehistoric man, especially as they are concentrated in the area of Ang-ang-hsi (Tsitsihar). Altogether sixteen living sites have been found arranged topographically in two rows—along the Nonni River and near the interior lakes. Although the area is generally dry, during the late summer it suffers torrential rains which transform the river into a violent flooding "sea" of water. Some of the prehistoric sites are found on old terraces which are frequently submerged. However, stratigraphy at these sites, and at Shabarakh Usu in Mongolia, shows that when man inhabited these sites the climate was milder and rainier than at present, fresh water lakes were plentiful, and forests grew where today there is only grassland. The fauna associated with man in 3000 B.C. included deer, boar, gazelle, fox, wolf, and hare—animals of the steppe and woodlands.

The tool kits of the people living at that time reflect and categorize the diversity of microenvironments they successfully inhabited. The Ang-ang-hsi tradition is clearly affiliated with that of the Shilka Valley and Baikal area in which the "microcore" technique of tool preparation predominates. The stoneworker prepared prismatic and conical cores by removing one or two flakes from a trihedral blank and then struck knife-like blades from these cores.

The people of the northern Tungpei shared a taiga way of life with the tribes of the Baikal. The great quantity of their food refuse is made up largely of fishbones and the shells of river mollusks. However, they had also begun to exploit the resources of the grasslands; grinding slabs and semi-lunar grinding stones appear along with the flint implements. The technology of Ang-ang-hsi brought the population, through extensive gathering of vegetal foods, into contact with an entirely different environment. This pattern was to be repeated several times in the history of the northern Tungpei as the forest people moved out onto the grasslands. Agriculture did not usually spread into the region but came as the result of very tentative experimentation, as the knowledge of cultivation, derived from the south, challenged a secure forest efficiency with a technologically and environmentally acceptable alternative.

CENTRAL ASIA

The distinct physiographic region of Central Asia is characterized by vast steppelands, volcanic plateaus, and sun-scorched deserts. Steppe vegetation covers much of the mountainous region as well as the plain, although there are some woodland belts along rivers. The quality of the environment has changed over the millennia, and the archeologist can suggest that the expansive wind-blown deposits of the past, sometimes accumulating in dune formations of over thirty feet, were piled up at a time when the depressions of the desert held bodies of water. It is as these old, dead sand dunes are eroding away that the artifacts of prehistoric men weather out and appear on the floor of the desert. Many explorers and archeologists have described the abundance of stone tools, remains of campsites and perhaps small temporary villages of steppe-dwellers who hunted small non-gregarious game with remarkably fashioned weapons—arrows tipped with small points made of blades detached from prismatic cores. The "microlithic" inventory of the steppe-desert lands included many compound tools such as scrapers, knives, and perforators, but also large flake tools and grinding implements. Many of the grinding slabs are worn quite thin with use, indicating that the subsistence technology incorporated the essential components of the environment through an appropriate response, one which proved effective and long-lasting. Whether casual cultivation of plants occurred, or simple encouragement of plants routinely gathered, the intense local elaborations seen in the cultures of the steppe had deep roots, nourished by the security of their relations with the environment. This quality of being "at home" is communicated by prehistoric recognition of raw materials which express the unique environment—the lovely rings made of ostrich egg shell; the beautiful chalcedony, agate, and jaspar pebbles, chosen, one might think, for their brilliant colors and worked with a masterful technique so that light refracted from their many facets.

The sand dunes of the Ordos region stretch, in a discontinuous pattern, down into eastern Shensi Province. Here in the area of Chao-i hsien and Ta-li hsien, the exposed and rolled artifacts of an early time have been found scattered over the surface. In most respects the "efficiency" of the desert-steppe dwellers of the Gobi and Central Asia was shared by peoples living in ecologically equivalent regions of China. It may eventually be possible to trace this technology south, through the grassland corridor leading into western Szechwan. One can expect to see it corresponding to the distribution of Tibetan fauna, fingering along the eastern-most slopes of the plateau. At least one reported find of yak bones and microblades may relate this western mountain zone to late sites in Kansu (Lohant'ang and Taip'ingkou) and to the cave sites of northwestern Yunnan.

SOUTHEAST ASIA

The topography of mainland Southeast Asia may be superficially characterized by its rivers, each individually framed by a double ring of mountains, its deltas and alluvial coasts. The early vegetation cover of tropical forests and parkland grew on primarily acidic red soils. Consistent with the topography, the forest efficiency of Southeast Asia developed in the two major ecological spheres of hill country and riverine seacoasts.

The radical difference in tool kits which contrasts the south with the north (i.e., the absence of microliths in the south) should not disguise the similarities of subsistence response.

1. Excavation at PanP'o, an early farming village. Shensi province.

2–3. (Above and opposite) Pottery from the site of PanP'o, showing the fish motif in full and "dissolved" representations. Black on redware.

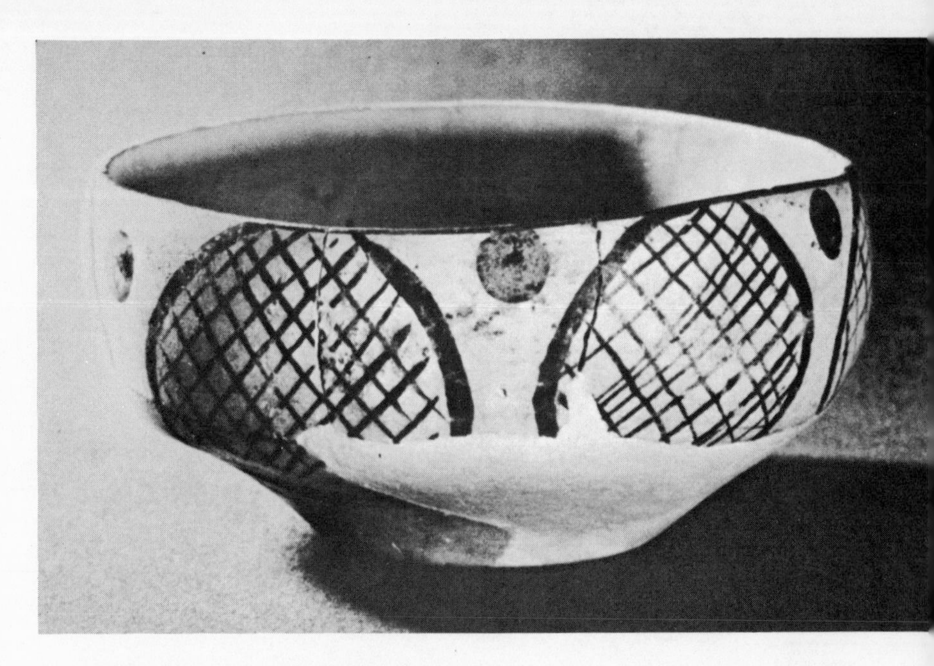

4. Pottery cup from Miao Ti Kuo in Honan province. Black on buff-ware; about 2½″ tall and 5″ in diameter. From Takeshi Sekino, *Arts of China, Neolithic Cultures to the T'ang Dynasty*, © 1968 by Kodansha International, Ltd.

5. Red pottery jar from Miao Ti Kuo with relief figure of lizard. From Takeshi Sekino, *Arts of China, Neolithic Cultures to the T'ang Dynasty*, © 1968 by Kodansha International, Ltd.

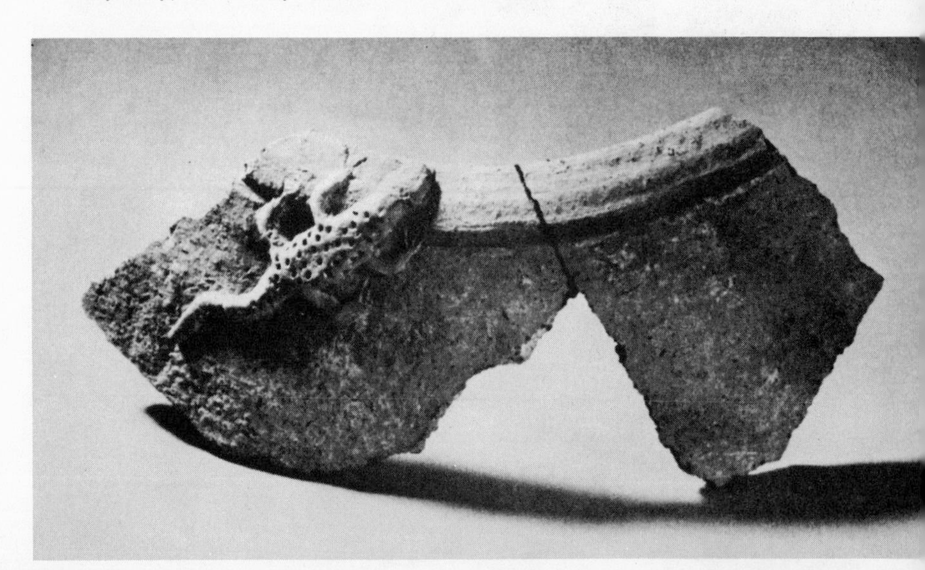

6. Pan Shan pottery urn, Kansu province. Black on red.

7. Detail from the handle, Ssu Mu Wu Ting bronze vessel. From Takeshi Sekino, *Arts of China, Neolithic Cultures to the T'ang Dynasty*, © 1968 by Kodansha International, Ltd.

8. Carved stone "fantastic" animal. Anyang, Honan province.

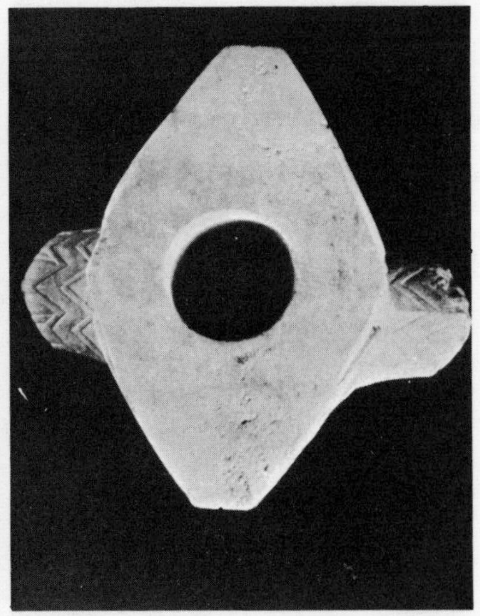

9. Carved stone "fantastic" animals. Anyang, Honan province.

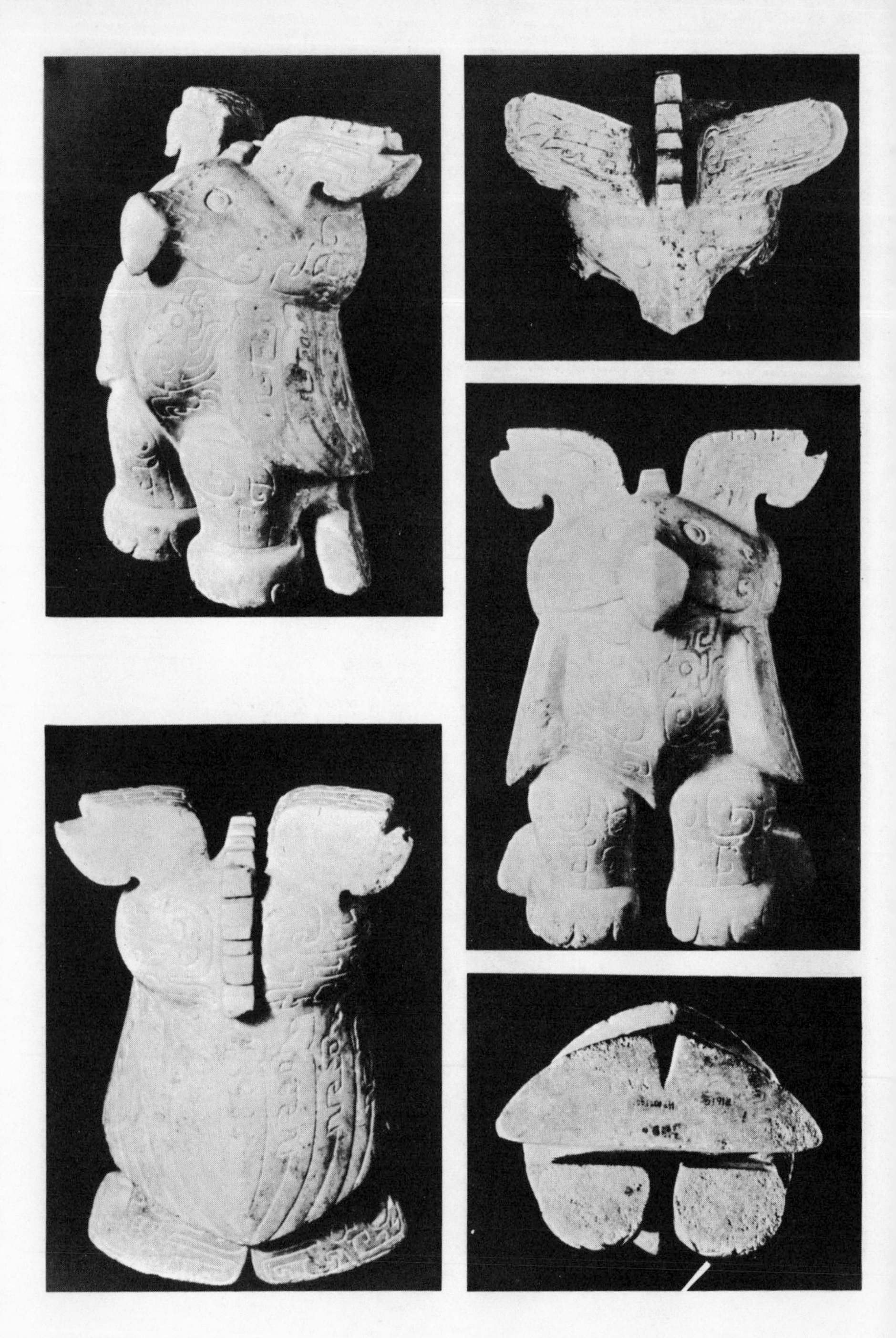

10. Carved stone "fantastic" animals. Anyang, Honan province.

The tools of Southeast Asia do not differ markedly from the pebble and flake implements of the Paleolithic which persist in some cases into the Iron Age. One cannot walk for long in the forests of Southeast Asia without becoming aware of the presence of the bamboo growth that gives such a remarkable texture to the environment. It is highly probable that the most widely used material of the tropical forest was bamboo, which is easily fashioned into a wide range of efficient tools. The medium of bamboo is extremely flexible and has been creatively worked into the material cultures of Southeast Asia as cutting-implements, body adornments, rafts, house frames, cooking utensils, containers, and musical instruments.

During the period characterized by the forest efficiency, people apparently lived more frequently in rock shelters than in open settlements. These cave dwellings were usually located near streams which provided a rich source of food—mollusks and fish—and easily found river pebbles that could be quickly flaked into heavy tools, and just as easily discarded. The mollusk shells were also used as tools and often shaped into rings and beads. The shellfish gatherers hunted, although not intensively. The bones of deer and wild boar and also of elephant and rhinoceros are found in the refuse. We must imagine that the last two were not actively pursued as game but were trapped or "come upon" in almost accidental fashion. Hunting did, in some instances, increase with time, perhaps influenced by microenvironmental changes in fauna. The pottery of the forest efficiency is handmade, often using the paddle-and-anvil technique, decorated with incised designs and cord and mat impressions. The subsistence technology had a dual focus—one on riverine produce and one on the forest itself. Plant consumption included many kinds of wild or tended nut trees (some varieties such as candlenut perhaps were used as fuel for lighting the interior of the cave home, and some, such as betel, were used as stimulants), bottle gourds and cucumbers, peas and beans, water chestnuts and even pepper.

SOUTH CHINA

The late persistence of this way of life and perhaps its resistance to agriculture (before the introduction of iron tools) is especially notable in the northern zone including much of South China. The most obvious feature of the topography of South China is the almost complete absence of plain or plateau, with the exception of the Chengtu alluvial fan (less than 10 per cent of the area), the area around Tungting and Poyang lakes, the marshy flats around Hankow and the Yangtze delta itself. The Yangtze cuts its way across hard rock ridges and the imposing mountains, cutting lengthy and precipitous gorges before it finally meanders towards the sea, forming many bow-shaped lakes and building its delta. The climate and vegetation of South China are largely determined by altitudinal variations: an alpine zone mixed with the remnants of coniferous forests above 3500 meters, a belt of the famous rhododendron and coniferous trees above 1650 meters and a rain forest of broad-leaf evergreens and oak above 1600 meters. The valley climate is warm and mild, supporting a native growth of bamboo and palm, tung-oil and fruit-bearing trees. Today the area still contains 39 per cent of the entire country's expanding forest.

In the southwest (Szechwan in particular) settlements were situated on the terraces of smaller streams, many of them tributaries of the Yangtze. Cemeteries were sometimes associated with the sites, and there is sufficient depth of occupational debris to support an inference of semi- or even fully-sedentary village life. The people hunted the game of the temperate forests and probably collected wild fruits and plants. More than anything else, intensive shellfish gathering and fishing sustained the population. Not only are there very impressive shell middens, but literally thousands of net-sinkers have been found in the refuse. The stone-pebble axes and adzes and flake-scrapers are essentially woodworking tools, probably used in constructing rafts or boats (one can suspect that the hide-covered coracle has great antiquity in Yangtze navigation), for making bamboo implements and for stripping bark or fibrous plants to make cordage for nets. The broad stone "hoes" or "spades" that are frequently found may have been used to excavate dwelling pits and clearings in front of cave shelters. No house remains have been found. Stone querns, mortars and pestles were not found, so wooden implements may have been used in the preparation of foods.

In the great gorges—the source of much raw material—workshops have been discovered in which unfinished rough-outs and unifacially worked pebbles abound. The tool makers of this region were very well acquainted with their materials, expending the minimum amount of labor on granular, igneous rocks which would obviously not take much wear. It almost appears as though the artisans chose pebbles which were "prepolished" by water action and only required gross chipping to achieve the correct shape for hafting, and minimum grinding to sharpen the cutting edge.

A similar series of sites have been located in the Tien ch'ih lake region of Yunnan Province, where a shellfish collecting subsistence supported small settlements of people prior to the introduction of wheat cultivation or while cultivation was in the "experimental" stage. Another extremely important site, but one which thus far stands alone in Southeastern China, is Hsi-chiao-shan, in Kwangtung. This hilltop site, surrounded in prehistoric times by freshwater ponds and streams, hints at a microlithic forest efficiency which may be more closely related to what is now the island Pacific than to the north.

The style of life that we have been describing has sometimes been called "Mesolithic," sometimes the period of "terminal hunting and gathering." We have preferred to use the term "forest efficiency," which emphasizes not stages of development, but the technology—cognitive, social and material—of human adaptation in prehistory.[1]

The gaps must of course be filled in with imagination, but to speak of forest efficiency is to remind us that the food gatherer knew every bush and stone of his terrain, knew the seasonal growth pattern of the mollusks and small animals, the migration and nesting habits of birds, and when to expect the fruiting of the trees. He, unlike the Paleolithic hunter, must have practiced some form of animal and vegetable conservation; in the manufacture of pottery he manipulated materials so that chemical transformation took place; with domesticated dogs he harnessed energy other than his own; with composite tools he began to explore the range of flexibility of raw materials and to solve more specialized technological problems. The ground work of the Neolithic revolution was prepared in the forest. The extraordinary paucity of artifactual remains is unfortunate: this was a time of human creativity and freedom, when the hesitant steps of the Paleolithic became firm and man settled into the world with confidence. The "bare landscape" became a laboratory for experimentation and choice of alternatives. From a technology that is "at one" with the environment the prehistoric societies that chose to elaborate the agricultural way of life developed a technology that confronts and competes with the environment.

The Agricultural Innovation

It is very difficult as yet to trace the appearance of the agricultural innovation in the archeological record of China.

[1] It is obvious that the American "tradition" of archeology, which relies heavily on ethnographic continuity and ecological interpretation, is best suited to this approach.

Without a doubt the "invention" took place many times, in many places. We have already seen the possible cultivation of nut trees and vegetables in Southeast Asia and can well imagine the encouragement of many plants, especially grasses, in the Tungpei forests. However, we are looking for a village farming efficiency that categorizes the environment in an entirely new way, with a new technology. The technology of efficient agriculture no longer deals with the environment of natural vegetation except as an indicator of fertility. The significant environment is made up of soils and water. The human carrying capacity of land is interpreted in terms of the "staying power" of the soil and its cultivability.

NORTHERN CHINA: SEED-CULTIVATION

In choosing the environment in which the agricultural experiment could succeed, early farmers in Asia avoided the dense, deciduous tree growth of the mountains and hills and settled on the loess terraces of the rivers of Northern China, especially the middle Huang and Wei river tributaries. Here they were assured of good drainage but had to cope with unpredictable fluctuations in rainfall. The natural vegetation cover of tall grasses and open mixed deciduous and coniferous forests presented certain technological problems to these farmers; the extensive root systems of the grasses were especially difficult. In the absence of a plow, a simple method of dibbling must have been used. The dibble has continued in use in contemporary times when planting vegetables, peas, and wheat. The numerous polished stone axes and adzes in the tool kit of early farmers suggests that they did clear some forest land for cultivation. At the one site for which a pollen column has been reported, the flora is a typical temperate (cool and dry) combination of grasses, club-moss, shrubs, birch, willow, oak, elm, and evergreens. Although ash lenses are not reported, it is probable that fire was one of the chief means of clearing off felled trees and shrubs and even dry grasses. In a time and place of unlimited land and small populations, swidden cultivation—i.e., shifting fields—did not entail shifting settlements. The multiplicity of ecological zones which the farming efficiency simultaneously occupied would have operated against moving a community from place to place as the soil fertility was depleted.

Fishing continued to play an extremely important role in the subsistence technology, witnessed archeologically by fishhooks, gorges, and net-sinkers. In the painted pottery, fish were commonly used in design motifs. (The involvement with fish in the art style is complete—they swim about the body of the vessel, sometimes wholly natural, sometimes dissected and split apart, often the "parts" are dissolved into geometric forms and reunited by the eye of imagination.) Hunting small game such as deer and rodents was more important than in the forest adaptation. This is evident in the quantities of beautifully made bone arrow points and in the preponderance of fleshing or scraping tools of stone. There are ample remains of chestnuts, hazelnuts, and pine seeds reminding us that gathering activities continued to be significant. It is also probable that many "weed plants," notably the chenopods, were part of the dietary repertoire. The use of wild grasses for thatch, matting, and possibly for fuel would have encouraged intensive collecting. The groves of trees surrounding villages provided a niche for the most prominent domesticated animal—the pig. None of the houses had attached enclosures for animals, so the swine must have rooted in the woods. It is possible that ditches (reported to have surrounded at least one village) kept the pigs from roaming at will in the fields during the evening. These ditches may also have provided drainage for the village.

Two vital aspects of the technology of the forest efficiency were employed to reinterpret the environment of early farming. One was fire, mentioned above as the probable method of clearing land for cultivation and enriching it. Controlled fire played an important part in forest existence, where it may have been used to favor and even localize the growth of plants enjoyed by game species and the wild vegetable foods and berries consumed by humans. The second technological change was manipulating the grasses themselves. True domestication of plants involved moving them out of the ecological niche in which they were found growing wild, and fostering their accommodation and specialization to new environments. This was done primarily with the millets, especially foxtail millet (*Setaria Italica Beauv. bar. germanica Trin*) and kaoliang (*Andropogon sorghum Brot.*). Some weeds were probably cultivated for oil and were brought out of their original forest-steppe environment along with the millets. Although we cannot yet say where the millets were first domesticated, there is both legendary and continuing ritualistic celebration of millet cultivation in China, evidencing very long familiarity and dependence. The nutritive qualities of these grains rank as high as wheat, and the stems (especially of the larger varieties) even today are used extensively for thatch and fuel. The millets are quick maturing and drought resistant, thus making them viable in the northern part of China, the Tungpei region, and later in the mountainous zone as well. An individual can be sustained on two to four pounds of millet per day when it is boiled as porridge or baked into cakes.

PAN P'O-T'SUN

We can glimpse this life through a remarkable series of excavations at the site of Pan P'o in southern Shensi. Pan P'o is representative of at least four hundred other known sites found on the loess terraces and along small streams of the Weishui valley. The village was large, about seventy thousand square meters including the settlement nucleus (itself about thirty thousand square meters in area) and the outer kiln and cemetery areas. A ditch surrounded the dwelling site, also enclosing many storage pits. (It has already been suggested that the ditch may have served a drainage function and also kept pigs from wandering into the fields, but the excavators of the site call it a "defense ditch.") At any moment in time the village may have held two hundred households with a population of between five hundred and six hundred. The houses were built of the most readily available materials—mud and straw and hewn logs. In the lifetime of the village, indeed of any given family, there was constant need to replenish, repair, and rebuild the houses. The house entrances all faced the south, probably out of consideration for prevailing cold, northerly winds. The low ceilinged entranceways also protected the inhabitants during the windy winters, and heating the interior of the house was often achieved by a centrally placed fire-pit. The house floors were excavated into the ground and carefully plastered with mud, and the roof supports were put into clay-lined postholes.

There were two styles of building, roughly clustered in separate areas of the village. The larger, rectangular house had a living space that averaged about twenty square meters, room enough for a family of four! The smaller, circular house usually had an interrupted floor-plan with low partitions, perhaps separating eating and sleeping areas. In the center of the village there was one very large structure, estimated to have covered at least 160 square meters. This building, more permanent than the others, had a foundation wall of fired earth one-half meter high. The posts that supported the roof were secured in this wall. The function of this structure is unclear. There were also two open sheds, which may have sheltered animals, or served as a drying shed for pottery, animal-skins, and fish.

We can people this ancient village, see the women chopping straw and stamping it into mud puddles to make the

Fig. 2 Reconstruction of houses in the village site of Pan P'o (see also Fig. 3)

materials for a house-raising; see them quietly sitting outside their homes pounding the grain for each day's food, softening and sewing the leather garments, perhaps grinding the pigments to be used in decorating the pottery, and tending the small gardens that were around and between the houses. Hunting and fishing were the work of men, perhaps of children also; children must have accompanied their families into the fields when field-clearing and harvesting required concentrated spurts of labor. It is possible that families camped in small thatch wind shelters during these busy seasons.

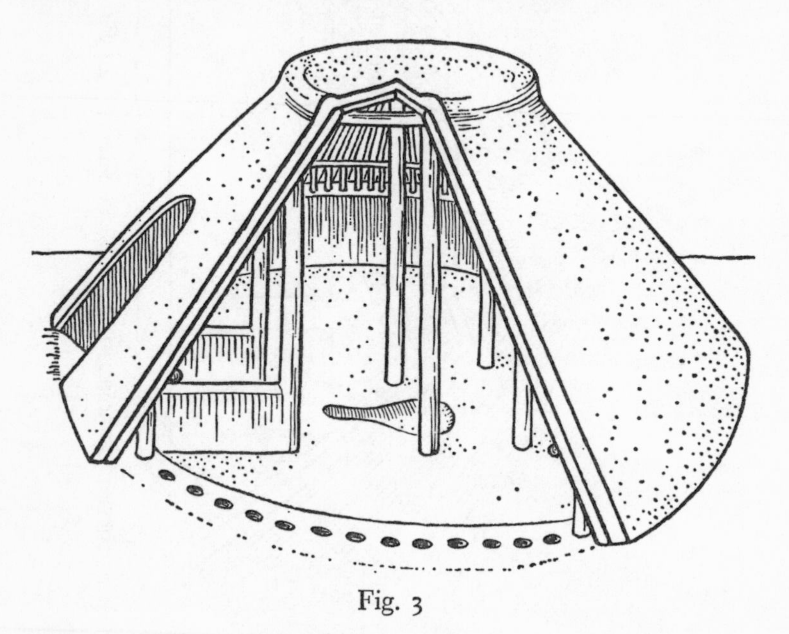

Fig. 3

An assured sedentary life provided the need for and time to produce all manner of containers—and probably tools or utensils—of basketry. But it was a fascination with pottery that best captures the village way of life at that time. This fascination was well expressed in the extraordinary variety of vessels—flat-bottomed, rounded, with supporting legs, with covers, spouts, handles—and the exuberance of decoration. Standing by themselves are the beautifully executed painted vessels—stirring perhaps the emotions of those who made them as much as the beholder. The continuity of design elements and the perfection of craftsmanship suggests that the designs were part of a heritage, perhaps traditionally transmitted through families of "good" artists rather than being part of the common pool into which the everyday ceramicist dipped. The contemporary meaningfulness of pottery was carried into the death ritual: almost all adult burials in the cemetery included one or more vessels placed carefully at the feet of the corpse.

The cemetery gives us our final glimpse of daily life. The children, who suffered the highest death rate, were placed in pottery urns and buried in amongst the houses, never fully separated from the family and home. The adult dead were buried in a specially reserved and probably sanctified area, but one which is a part of the village—the hallmark perhaps of a pattern of life that had come to incorporate the land into itself as the efficient farming technology increasingly rooted and held fast the people. In effect the earlier farmers of China made their first claim on the environment. This was probably a time of optimism, before the fragmentation of the cultivable land was a necessary social component of technology.

Pastoralism: a New Way of Life

Before leaving this discussion of technology and environment, brief mention must be made of another way of subsistence. This is the way of pastoralism, the prevailing mode on the vast Eurasian steppe, reaching, and at times overflowing, the North China plains. Pastoralism is a technology which defines a life-style and structures the ecosystem. Man, in his social aspect, the community, lives in symbiotic relationship with his animal herds within an ecological niche: the pasture. The herds supply nourishment, clothing, shelter, fuel, and prestige, and serve as a commodity. The herders supply protection, especially of the young, and extend the foraging range of the animals. The gradual shift in emphasis from the village farming efficiency to the pastoral efficiency took place in the parts of the grassy steppeland where uncertainty of rainfall and inability to cultivate without iron tools made total dependence on agriculture hazardous.

The agricultural village efficiency spread northeast and west, becoming fully realized and defined as it brought the basic innovation—seed cultivation—to the limits of its original ecological setting. We have already suggested that it became an "addition" to the basic forest efficiency of the Tungpei without dramatically altering the way of life until very early historic times. Between the second and first millennia, the grassland steppes and semi-arid regions of the Tungpei saw the growth of a bronze age which, although built on a diversified foundation, spread a kind of uniformity across Eurasia. To the north it reached Lake Baikal, during the Andronovo-Karasuk it reached Europe, and during the period called Western Chou it moved into China as well. The tribal basis for the steppe barbarians was established as more intensive agricultural activities developed. Stone plowshares were replaced by bronze on plows pulled by draft animals. (Horses and oxen were used for labor, but probably eaten as well.) A local metallurgical industry manufactured bronze agricultural implements such as sickles and knives, as well as ornaments. Settlements were large—some were 50,000–52,000 square meters in area and generally located on hilltops. The farmers utilized natural drainage patterns to foster the growth of millet on the slopes. Sheep were raised (at least in Jehol) for wool and meat.

The self-containment of settlements disappeared as this way of life, which came to be known archeologically as the "slab-burial culture" impressed certain stylistic patterns of behavior over the previous multi-focused regional pattern.

The seed-cropping complex continued to fill up the available landscape of riverine terraces and easily-worked loessland. In eastern Kansu, accommodations to semi-aridity were made, resembling those of the southern Tungpei. In addition to millet cultivation, the domestication of animals, especially cattle and sheep, became increasingly important to the economy. Copper implements were added to the tool inventory: awls, knives, chisels, and ornaments were made of this metal. As in the Tungpei, the people of Ch'i Chia in Kansu frequently used the medium of bone rather than stone to work out many tool problems. The emphasis on animal domestication and use of metals indicates that the farming efficiency did not become well established and that another path of subsistence adaptation was chosen.

The breakdown, or transition, from the village farming efficiency appeared in Eurasia as the agriculturist, unable to fully conquer the grasslands, found the nomadic herding way of life (facilitated by the domestication of the horse) a more efficient adaptation. First seen in the Tripolye complex at the western end of the steppe-desert corridor (perhaps as early as 3500 B.C.), the conjunction of cattle-sheep-horse-breeding with agriculture appears in the Upper Yenesei basin of Siberia, where it continued to flourish until the first millennium B.C. In the Minusinsk region, where mining activities became increasingly important (copper, tin, and gold), large agricultural villages disappear from the archeological record and only thin cultural deposits of debris remain to testify to prehistoric occupation. The most prominent aspect of this culture comes from the graves, which themselves have architectural qualities. They are stone-lined cists, and in them are found not only the bones of humans, but of sheep, horses, and camels. The nomadic character of life as the people moved through the pasturelands with their herds is graphically highlighted by a Karasuk stele on which is engraved a horse-drawn covered wagon. In these wagons, perhaps the "home" of each small family during its period of wandering, one could probably have found large pots containing the millet and barley upon which the people fed and the small bronze knives with which they performed their daily chores. Their chariots will be seen again when we discuss the Royal Tomb burials of the Shang.

PRELUDE

The self-contained quality of the village farming efficiency persisted, and the approach to the environment was essentially multi-focused. The agricultural way of life began in an ecologically diversified zone, where it was not rigidified. By continuing to exploit a full range of resources the loessland villagers were assured security of subsistence but were handicapped in the sense that the same fluidity hampered urbanization. Only after the agricultural innovation was brought out of this zone did it begin to take root, but a technological approach to the land involving the use of iron was necessary before it could be brought to fruition. There was a long way to go before the characteristic picture could be painted: the naked rocks, the mountaintops, the trees, and the fields with tiny creatures moving about them; men and water buffalo as much a part of the landscape as the mists, the smoke of the cooking fires, and the butterflies.

Chinese "civilization" was postponed till much later in time and can be recognized only when it takes on the Oriental characteristics familiar to us from Mesopotamia. Not until the time of Chou does this pattern of urbanization emerge —the densely populated centers of craft specialization and commerce supported by labor-intensive agriculture. But we will return to this in a later chapter.

CHAPTER III

Village and Farmer

Viewing China at the relative "moment" when the agricultural way of life restructured the landscape in its own cultural terms, we are forced to look at the microsystems of ecological adaptation. Although discussing what is usually called the Neolithic, this technological viewpoint permits us to escape the restrictions of artificial "stages of development" or historical "periods" of time. In reality, the mosaic patterning of the cultural landscape which emerged during the Neolithic persists and underlies all subsequent movements of Chinese history, for it necessarily preceded the creation of the peasant.

Frequently the tiles of the mosaic seem to be repetitive, but they are never identical. Although pervasive "styles" may wash over large areas—and in many instances these are but functions of the retrospective view of the archeologist—the similarities are structural concomitants of the technological approach to the enviornment represented by village agriculture. For not only does the technology of agriculture reorganize space in terms of bounded fields and incorporated settlements, but it reorganizes time—new meanings are given to the passing of seasons and diurnal alternations—and so it affects the individual human being.

In the sixth month we eat wild plums and cherries,
In the seventh month we boil mallows and beans.
In the eighth month we dry the dates,
In the tenth month we take the rice
To make with it the spring wine,
So that we may be granted long life.
In the seventh month we eat melons,
In the eighth month we cut the gourds,
In the ninth month we take the seeding hemp,
We gather bitter herbs, we cut the ailanto for firewood,
That our husbandmen may eat.

In the ninth month we make ready the stackyards,
In the tenth month we bring in the harvest,
Millet for wine, millet for cooking, the early and the late,
Paddy and hemp, beans and wheat.
Come, my husbandmen,
My harvesting is over,
Go up and begin your work in the house,
In the morning gather thatch-reeds,
In the evening twist rope;
Go quickly on to the roofs.
Soon you will be beginning to sow your many grains.

In the days of the second they cut the ice with tingling blows;
In the days of the third they bring it into the cold shed.
In the days of the fourth very early
They offer lambs and garlic.
In the ninth month are shrewd frosts;
In the tenth month they clear the stackgrounds.
With twin pitchers they hold the village feast,
Killing for it a young lamb.
Up they go into their lord's hall,
Raise the drinking-cup of buffalo-horn:
'Hurray for our lord; may he live for ever and ever!'

Shih Ching
(translation after Waley, 1937)

The villagers of the north (Honan, Shensi, and Shansi) had three ecosystems within which they organized the intersecting activities of their lives: the plains along the Huang, the Wei, and the Fen rivers and their smaller tributaries, the shrub- and tree-covered mountain slopes and the streams themselves.

The relevant factors of the agricultural ecosystem are soil and climate. The soil, as noted earlier, is loessic (primary in the west, derived in the east) and therefore both rich and unresistant to the labors of the cultivator. The climate is created by the topography of the land—the Tsinling mountain chain bars the moist winds from the Pacific so that precipitation rarely is greater than twenty inches per year. From January to June the cold of Siberia penetrates, from July through August the rains pound and flash floods cut deeply as the waters pour down from the western mountains.

It is possible, by moving carefully and selectively through the wealth of data from prehistoric sites (well over one thousand) attributable to the Neolithic of this northern region of China, to trace the involvement of land into the ecosystem of agriculture.

MIAO TI KUO

Stratigraphically later than the Pan P'o village described earlier, the site of Miao Ti Kuo is in Honan Province (near the city of Shen-hsien) but in the same river basin-loessland system. The two prehistoric villages[1] of Miao Ti Kuo and San Li Ch'iao are situated across from each other on the north and south terraces of the river Ch'ing Lung.

The people of these villages, and of the hundreds of contemporary villages that blossomed in profusion along the

[1] Although cultural debris is scattered over a very large area (24,000 and 180,000 square meters respectively), it is difficult to interpret the pattern of settlement because few house remains were found. The overwhelming portion of artifacts came from the excavated "ash pits."

many small tributaries of the Huangho, filled the gentle valleys with the business of their lives. (Figure 4) For many generations they continued to clear the fields with fire and stone hoes, and to cultivate the rich soil with forked wooden implements and antler digging tools. The land yielded to their manipulation, water was in most years sufficient for plant growth and not often destructive in its abundance; increasingly the people came to depend upon agriculture for

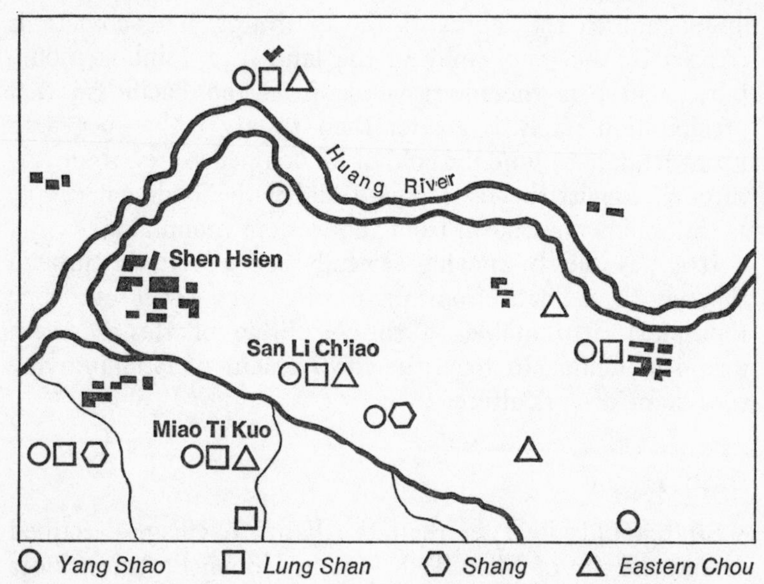

Fig. 4 Archeological sites in the region of Shen Hsien, Honan Province

their subsistence. This confidence is reflected in the extraordinary painted designs of their pottery: here a lizard or frog to remind us of the river, there a bird—perhaps snared or shot with a delicately worked bone arrow point, but overwhelmingly the curvilinear representations are of vegetation, of flowers and leaves.

The fine designs, often executed in combined negative and positive modes, were painted in black on red pottery. The vessels were fired in the several kilns that were located in the village. As the work of highly skilled artists became known and desired, one can imagine that some pottery was circulated among villages. The impressive array of small ornaments, rings of polished stone, mother-of-pearl, and pottery, pendants of turquoise and shell, necklaces of pottery beads, hairpins and combs of bone, seems also to indicate a kind of petty trade.

At the time of its earliest occupation, the people of Miao Ti Kuo built rather large, rectangular houses. They excavated shallow pits of six by seven meters and dug narrow, sloping, south entrance corridors. This arrangement trapped the bitter winds of winter and helped preserve the interior warmth. The floor itself was carefully compacted of mud,

Fig. 5 Reconstructed houses in the village of Miao Ti Kuo (see also Fig. 6)

chopped straw, and powdered burnt clay. After it had dried, it was polished to a smoothness. Strong poles were implanted all around the edges of the pit and the mud walls were built up to the roof. The roof itself was pyramidal in shape, supported by four center posts. An oven was situated near the entranceway to provide further heating. Storage pits dotted the house environs, and the debris of everyday living—broken artifacts, fish and deer bones—was dumped into ash pits.

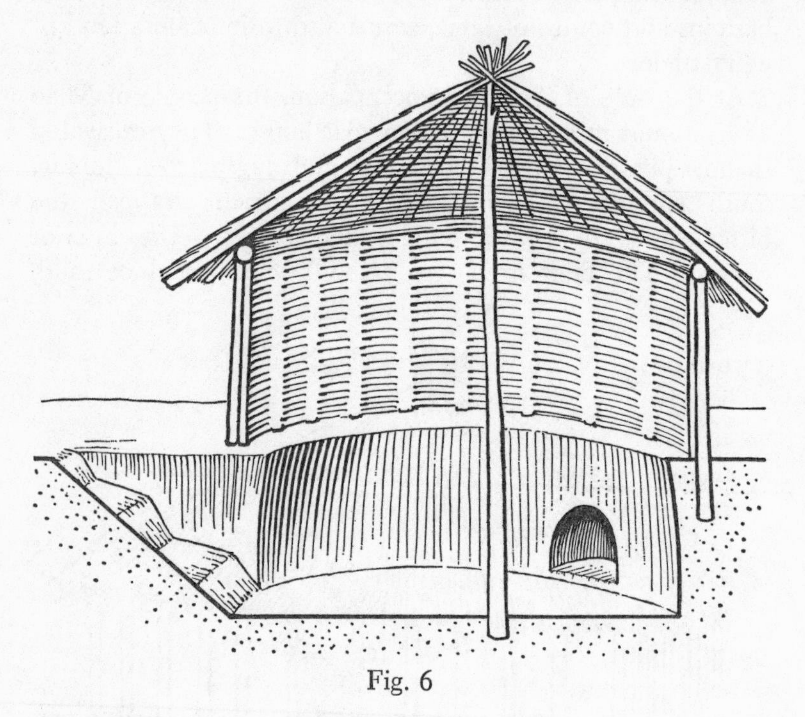

Fig. 6

As time passed, it became the custom to build much smaller houses, round with deeply excavated entranceways. Although it is impossible to guess what social changes were occurring, there is an increasing sense of "boundedness" that accompanies the succeeding developments. There are ditches running through the village; domesticated pigs, goats, and cattle appear, signifying containment. The refuse and storage pits are of uniform "pocket" shape and were distributed in a very orderly manner. The dead were buried in a cemetery, row upon row.

People's attention turned inward toward intensified agricultural and domestic labors; they spent much more time in the fields, using new implements for digging, and stone knives and sickles for reaping the harvest. The long winter evenings were spent sitting near the wall-fireplace, twining and twisting the fibres of baskets and mats, spinning the yarns of hemp for woven garments. The exuberant painted pottery is infrequently seen; perhaps the utilitarian hand-made grey ware was entirely a household product, fired in the communal village kiln. It is only at the very end of the occupation of Miao Ti Kuo-San Li Ch'iao that a small percentage of the pots are manufactured with the wheel, and the vessel shapes at this time—the *kuei*, the handled *li*-tripod, and the steamers—already preshadow the influence of Chou styles.

There is no question but that the sites of this region show a continuous and self-contained development. There is no evidence of population movements, apart from the constant small-scale budding off of tiny hamlets; almost everywhere the earlier occupations, sometimes called Yangshao, are associated with the later, often called Lungshan.

The pattern of productive technology was established during this period, and with it the essential relationship of men and environment. What was soon to change was the social organization of the distributive and manufacturing economy, and with that came the attitudes and values of civilization. The outlines of this transformation, which probably began about 1800 B.C., can be seen in the many "late Neolithic" sites of northwestern Honan, along the southern tributaries of the Huang and upper Huai drainage system.

EHR LI-T'OU

In western Honan Province, Yenshih County, there are numbers of sites which exhibit the social rearrangements that signalled the breakdown of self-sufficiency of the Neolithic villages and the beginnings of a new technological pattern. Here, on the edges of the great Huangho plain, the agricultural innovation matured as the farmers tackled the soils that were to yield five thousand harvests. Here the intensity of careful cultivation, the enriching techniques of fertilization with human wastes, and the concentration of human labor wrested more certain crop yields from the soil. Villages were not isolated, but were rapidly springing up along all the tributaries of the Huang, tying the little valleys into a network of communication and circulation of goods.

At the site of Ehr Li-T'ou, there is a hint of the beginnings of town life, a busy commerce in commodities and manufactures (but still not in the products of the soil) and a differentiation of economic roles. One very large structure of about one hundred square meters in area was built with a stamped earth foundation floor and sheltering walls of wattle and daub. Nearby were clusters of small houses, kilns, water wells, and storage pits. Whether the large building housed a wealthy family or was itself the focus of market activities is not known, but the kinds of goods found in the numerous rich burials suggest the latter. The manufacture of simple bronze objects (knives, a bell, pins, and fishhooks) in the town itself means that at least one family was initiated in the specialized occupation of metalworking and that other families were able to obtain the necessary raw materials and purchase the products of this artisanship. Pottery manufacture had also developed into a highly specialized craft, vessels were often wheel-made, decorated with complex repetitive motifs, incised and often stamped; ritually prescribed shapes were made for ceremonies and burials. A number of human skeletons were inexplicably mutilated or buried with the hands tied before death. They symbolize, perhaps, the emergence of an elite (economic or religious) which could command the lives of others.

KANSU: THE T'AO RIVER VALLEY

Along the banks of the T'ao River (a western tributary of the Huangho) the low-lying loessial terraces are intersected by many ancient ravines and gullies. During the period of earliest agricultural occupation numerous little villages were scattered along the terraces, overlooking the broad river valley.

Although there is no primary evidence of prehistoric agriculture, the location of the villages and twentieth-century cultivation practice suggest that rainfall was sufficient to sustain the growing of millet in the hills and vegetables on the river plain. However, the wide range of non-domesticated animals (several species of deer and cattle), the flourishing bone manufacture of arrow points, awls, needles, chisels, and ornaments show an intensive exploration of another ecology, dominated by the collecting and hunting of naturally occurring rather than domesticated species. No architectural features remain at these sites, but the depth of the ashy floor-layers (sometimes over two meters deep) testifies to a stability of occupation that must have spanned considerable time.

The generations of inhabitants were isolated by the topography of the region. One can imagine the tracery of worn footpaths between villages, a communication network of kinship relations—the marriage processions, messages of births and deaths that leapt across the natural barriers—but the villages were economically self-contained. For a long time to come there were to be no market towns to organize the circulation of produce and goods, no urban satellites to impose the administrative will of the political center. The sole unifying force that broke through the endlessly repetitive pattern of village life was the intensely stylized death ritual, itself a reaffirmation of the regenerative thread of kinship. High in the Pan Shan hills, sometimes as far as twenty kilometers distant from the settlements, were five great cemeteries. Here, in a final conquest of the landscape, the dead of many villages of the river valley were buried with the fantastic painted urns that were especially made for the ceremony. Perhaps the famous ceramic heads hint at the drama: are they the masks that were carried by the mourners, or were the dead painted with rich unnatural decoration before interment?

The ecosystem which focused on animal exploitation became increasingly dominant as the desert-like conditions of soil and climate continued to retard intensification of the agricultural way of life. Villages could expand neither in size nor in density of distribution; rather, more people became involved in tending herds of now-domesticated cattle, sheep, and goats. A social pattern of semi-nomadism adapted to the grazing behaviors of these animals was merged with sedentary farming and many "Neolithic" elements were reformulated.

We cannot say whether animal husbandry was the responsibility of small families, certain lineages, or simply specialized individuals, but the economic involvement with their mixed herds is made very evident by the incorporation of animal bones into sacred procedures and activities. The abundant use of cattle and sheep scapulae in divination was but one aspect of this involvement; we cannot possibly interpret the widespread incorporation of pig jawbones in human burials.

The pottery which is widely distributed in eastern Kansu, Ninghsia, and even Inner Mongolia at this time (called the "Ch'i Chia" pottery) was no longer painted. A major aesthetic investment was put into shaping the vessels; many forms are reminiscent of skin containers and the predominant feature is the large looped handle.

In the course of wandering about the countryside, perhaps while herding their animals, copper nuggets were discovered and brought back to encampments and villages. The metal was treated as another variety of stone and hammered into simple knives, awls, and rings. There are burying grounds within the villages, and a few of the graves contain two skeletons, a man and a woman.

The spirit of fragmentation and mobility which begins to pervade the region at the time of Ch'i Chia is increasingly expressed in the multiplicity of ceramic art styles, the small-scale circulation of bronze and stone ornaments that, by about 1000 B.C., seemed to reach from the steppes of Central Asia to the hills of Shensi.

The pottery of this later time is coiled and beaten ware. It is painted in black on red and white-slipped backgrounds; bold, freewheeling designs swirl over the vessels, many of which have the typical large loop-handles. It is possible to trace out the artistic specialization of a dozen styles and lesser traditions in the treatment of pottery, and these have been given cultural labels such as Hsin Tien, T'ang Wang, Ssu Wa, and Sha Ching. Distinctive burial customs also reflect cultural behavior that may have reinforced the ethnicity of the many population groups occupying the region: Some practiced cremation, others treated their dead with red ochre, some preferred extended burials, others flexed the corpses into the fetal position.

At the site of K'e Hsing Chuang, near Sian, an excavated chronological sequence has demonstrated first the superposition of the Ch'i Chia over the earlier Neolithic, and then the emergence of a cultural complex which can be associated with the "Chou" people. The settlement is of unknown size, but only three thousand meters have been excavated. Within the village, the houses were stylistically uniform: rectangular single units and houses of two and three rooms are connected with passageways. The floors of the houses were paved with the compacted debris of long occupation. These remains again reveal the mixed economy that is the continuing hallmark of the region. The people engaged in millet agriculture, kept herds of sheep and cattle, and also domesticated dogs and pigs. The banks of the nearby streams were collecting grounds for rabbit and water deer, and the plentiful fish were taken on hooks made of bone. Very large pits (some are four meters square) are crammed with the refuse of these activities, but also contain human burials; a similar lack of stylistic or traditional rigidity is found in the pottery, which is not executed with great care or outstanding design. Although at the threshold of civilization, the signs of explosive transformation are peculiarly absent: one looks in vain for the intensity of focus and excitement which we think should accompany the emergence of civilization. In fact, the optimum involvement of the land into the ecology of agriculture was achieved on the Neolithic level of organization and could not advance any further. In the far west, the rearrangement of ecology emphasizing the pastoral alternative continued to develop, and merged with the Central Asian nomadic way of life.

RICE CULTIVATION

In the south, where we have seen a somewhat different aspect of the forest efficiency, it is difficult to perceive as yet the first appearance of farming villages. The economic pattern of fishing and planting (i.e. garden, root, and tree crops) continued late into historic time. It is certain that this "digging-stick" horticulture gradually increased in crop inventory and evolved into a complex tropical shifting agriculture.

We do not have any clear evidence for the early domestication of rice. Thus far its first appearance is in Eastern India, at about 2000 B.C.[2] The existence of a great many Sanscritic words designating rice in various states—in the husk, cooked, fried, flattened, etc.—testifies to its antiquity but tells us nothing of its origins. Recent botanical studies have suggested that the ancestor of *Oryza Sativa* (the rice cultivated in East Asia today) is *O. Perennis*, a deep-water wild rice found in India and Southeast Asia. If this proves to be the case, rice cultivation may have started in the swamps and marshes, where it was part of the basic forest efficiency. It did not emerge out of this ecological setting until specialized techniques of land manipulation were introduced, probably from the Near East.[3] These techniques involved the terracing of slopes to hold water and soil for wet-rice culture. The system of terrace building, field-levelling, plant selection, water control, seed-beds, and transplanting, the use of plow and harrow and sometimes the power of the water buffalo spread with relative slowness from a postulated Southeast Asian center, (Indo-China?) into the island world of the Pacific and northward through China. It reached Korea and Japan only in the seventh century A.D., and other areas even more recently.

THE HANSHUI VALLEY

The earliest indication of this complex appears in China about 1000 B.C. at the group of sites known as Ch'u Chia Ling in the Hanshui Valley. Here, however, it is incomplete, lack-

[2] Recent discoveries in Thailand suggest an even earlier date for rice domestication in Southeast Asia.

[3] However, rice is not easily moved. One of the important and controlling factors in the productivity of rice is the exposure to sunlight, and extensive breeding experimentation is necessary to make the necessary adaptations to differing patterns of cloud cover, seasonality, etc. This helps to explain the "lateness" of rice cultivation, since thorough familiarity with vegetation and techniques of domestication is implied in successful rice agriculture.

ing draft animals and plows, and it is uncertain that terracing took place.

On the middle Yangtze plain (of central Hupei and northern Hunan provinces) we can see at least one instance of this unfolding experiment as the addition of rice cultivation came to supplement an already efficient farming centered on millet.

Numerous small villages, situated on the river terraces and on small hillocks, came into existence at approximately the same time as the Huangho plains villages and represented a similar ecological strategy. The houses of the villages were small, round, and of earthen construction; the stone tools were the basic tools used for clearing the land and preparing the soil; rectangular and stepped axes, adzes, and scrapers were chipped and sometimes polished at the working edge. Simple designs were sometimes painted on pottery after it had been fired, but there was no elaboration of vessel shape or decoration. Although the villagers kept numerous pigs, they continued to hunt deer.

At some point in time (we can only suggest at about 1000 B.C.) preliminary manipulation of the rice plant began to succeed. The land was cleared with perforated and polished axes and adzes, and it was cultivated with thin, flat hoes. The same stone tools were probably used to build up shallow embankments to hold water during the early growing period and to prepare seed-beds. Much time was spent in the fields, especially when transplanting the new green shoots which required painstaking care. The rice was harvested with perforated polished knives of stone, and perhaps bamboo, that were strung around the wrist and grasped in the hand. After the harvest, the stalks of the plants were brought in from the fields to be stored for fuel and thatch. The winnowing and threshing of the grain may have been done in the fields or in the village; certainly the husked rice was spread to dry in the village streets before it was collected and stored. Some of the husks and chopped bits of rice straw were used to temper the clay out of which the house walls were built. The houses are quite large—sometimes 14 m x 5.6 m—and frequently have two rooms. The continuity of life was emphasized by the burials, almost always near the houses, which included grave goods.

Gradually the pottery of the Ch'u Chia Ling phase became more and more stylized as decorative techniques such as stamping, burnishing, and perforating the clay became perfected. Ornamental jewelry worked in fine stone, elaboration of weaving, and experimentation in pottery styles may well have reflected the spirit of innovation and vigor that accompanied the ethnic crystallization of a regional tradition.

With time, the domesticity of these farming villages is sculpturally symbolized in little clay figurines of numerous kinds of birds and animals, turtles and fish. Realistically modeled dogs, ducks and geese, and sheep with curled horns represent the familiar items of everyday life—as do the carefully prepared burials of children in mortuary urns.

THE LOWER YANGTZE VALLEY

The entire complex of wet-rice cultivation is first seen in South China at river-terrace and hill-slope sites in Kiangsi and Chekiang. We can sense a new approach to land-tilling which permits an explosion in the inventory of crops at the sites of Ch'ien Shan Yang in the Hangchow area. Many new agricultural tools were used, including the plow that was drawn by water buffalo. With stone plowshares, hoes, and spades, labor-intensive cultivation was possible but not fully realized. The fullest expression of human manipulation of land and water had to wait until the introduction of iron. However, together with remains of rice grains, there were peaches, melons, water chestnuts, sesame, and beans. Of special note, peanuts were grown by the farmers in Chekiang and Kiangsi. These must have been an important vegetable protein supplement to the animal diet of pork, venison, and boar. There is no archeological indication for field utilization practices, but we can hypothesize multiple-cropping on irrigated lands, and favored gathering locales and orchards in the hills. (Figure 7)

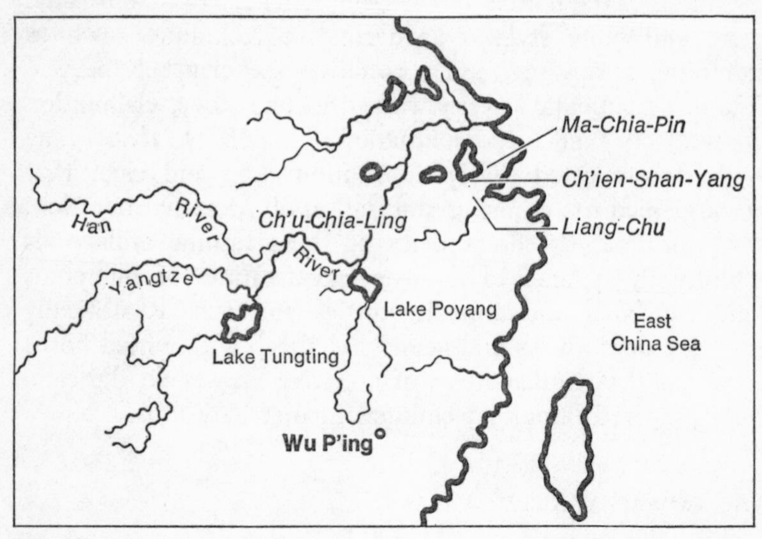

Fig. 7 Archeological sites in the Hanshui Valley and Lower Yangtze region

Gradually a specialized approach to the land emerged, and villages were built on hillocks and mounds that rise two to ten meters above the surrounding plain. The mounds were situated along the banks of rivers and lakes usually in clusters of up to sixteen; they were frequently artificially flattened on top and a few may have been terraced. The location of the villages suggests that rice farming pre-empted all other agricultural activities. The mound construction permitted the people to survive the floods that in their destructive rampages enriched and made fertile the soil. At the same time, proximity to the streams made it possible for the villagers to bring water to the rice fields during the droughts that occurred at the time of the very sensitive growing season.

The evidence for irrigation has not yet been revealed by archeological investigations, but certain literary allusions suggest that the counterweighted bailing-bucket was used at least as early as the fifth century B.C. to raise water from one level to another. A passage in the *Chuang Tzu* describes this device:

> Tzu-Kung had been wandering in the south in Ch'u, and was returning to Chin. As he passed a place north of the Han River, he saw an old man working in a garden. Having dug his channels he kept on going down into a well, and returning with water in a large jar. This caused him much expenditure of strength for very small results. Tzu-Kung said to him, "There is a contrivance (chieh) by means of which 100 plots of ground may be irrigated in one day. Little effort will thus accomplish much. Would you, sir, not like to try it?" Tzu-Kung said, "It is a lever made of wood, heavy behind and light in front. It raises water quickly so that it comes flowing into the ditch, gurgling in a steady foaming stream. Its name is the swape (kao)."

The methods of labor-intensive cultivation which characterize modern agriculture do not appear until after the fifth century. Two major requirements for labor-intensive cultivation had yet to be worked into agricultural technology: the invention and improvement of iron implements[4] and the use of animal labor harnessed to the plow. The most famous Chinese devices, such as the chain pump for raising water and irrigating fields, were not in use until early T'ang, and the noria (water wheel) was apparently not used until A.D. 200–300 or even later.

The specialization of techniques involved in the reinterpretation of environment by rice-growing cultures of the lower Yangtze region is accompanied by new patterns of social in-

[4] It should be noted, however, that the Ch'u of the Hanshui region were the first to effectively integrate iron into agricultural technology.

teraction. The settlements may represent small networks of social communication—kin and craft—and exchange. The individual units may have been unified by co-operative economic and agricultural endeavors, and some degree of specialization is indicated by the village-based production of bronze knives, arrow points, axes, and tripod vessels. The sense of emerging crystallization of an overarching ethnic identity is once again implicit in the pottery, the "geometric stamped ware" that was made and circulated throughout the southeast of China at this time. This ware, decorated with the impressions of paddles or medallions carved with linear designs, was made in workshops where the craftsmen worked a limited number of motifs into patterns that were traditionally recognized and enjoyed.

TOWARDS HISTORY

At the end of a famous section of the *Shu Ching, The Book of Documents*, the legendary Yü surveys the realm of China: on the east, dipping down to the sea, on the west, stretching into the moving sands, to the north and to the south, to the extent of the four seas it is filled with his fame and influence.[5] Just preceding this sentence (in the *Yü Kung*, or *Tribute of Yü*) there is a descriptive passage which is really a graphic map of the interior ordering of the realm:

(In the central kingdom) he conferred lands and names on those who were virtuous (and did not obstruct the emperor). Stretching for five hundred li in all directions from the capital were the fields in the service of the emperor. From the first hundred li of these, the people brought as revenue the whole plant (the grain and straw); from the second they brought

[5] It is the accepted view that the *Yü Kung* describes the lower valleys of the Huangho and Yangtze, with the plains area between them and also the Shantung Peninsula. To the west it covers the Wei and Han rivers, the southern parts of Shansi and Shensi. To preserve the feeling of the texts, the following translations are literal rather than literary.

only the closely cut ears; from the third they brought the straw; people in these three zones also perform other services. From the fourth hundred li the people brought grain in the husk, and from the fifth they brought the cleaned grain.

The next zone of five hundred li is the land of the nobility. In the first hundred li of this zone were the cities and lands of the high ministers and officers. The next zone is the area of "securing peace," the zone of pacification. In the first three hundred li, the people cultivate the lessons of learning and moral duties (i.e., become sinicized), but in the remaining area they devote themselves to warfare. In the next zone, the zone of allied barbarians (mostly Yi) extended for three hundred li, while the remainder was occupied by nomads. The outer zone constitutes the wild domain, occupied by the Man barbarians, and along its periphery are the nomads.

Indeed, this verbal diagram of concentric squares was the "view from within," the political model which symbolized the emergence of the Middle Kingdom and codified the structural arrangements by which it was extended.

It is interesting to note that this model, later to be reinterpreted in the mode of temple and palace architecture and even in city planning, is attached to the end of a work that is otherwise totally unpolitical. The *Yü Kung* is a remarkable piece of early geographic reportage. It is entirely naturalistic and permits us an extraordinary vision of the landscape of China as it was conceived before the political overlay of empire-building.

The *Yü Kung* is economic geography in the cultural sense: it describes the natural environment in terms of the prevailing technological relationships. The Chinese term for geography is *ti-li,* earth "pattern"; in other words, how the landscape is organized and consequently perceived. The inseparability of environment and technology is made abundantly clear in the description of the nine provinces: at the beginning of each there is a classification of soils which is defined by contextual phrases relating to crop yields (in terms of revenues), tribute (economic activities other than agriculture), and availability of water. Thus, "in the province of K'e Chou the soil was white and soft, its revenues were of the highest class and its fields of the middle class. The waters of the Heng and Wei were made to follow their proper courses and the Ta-lu was cultivated. The Niao Yi people also dwelt here, and they wore skin garments." In another province, Liang Chou, "the Min and Po mountains were cultivated, the T'o and Ts'un rivers were conducted in their proper channels and the Ts'ai-meng hills were regulated (laid out). The Ho Yi barbarians were affected by all this. Its soils were bluish-black, the fields of the highest of the lowest class. Its tribute was gold, iron, silver, steel, stones for arrow points, musical stones, black bears, brown and white bears, foxes and wildcats and articles woven with their hair. The felt-wearing barbarians of Si King follow the Huan river and come this way."

Finally, describing one more of the nine provinces, Sü Chou, where "the Huai and Yi rivers were regulated, the Meng and Yü mountains were cultivated. The marsh was drained into a lake and the plains were levelled. The soil was red, clayey and rich. Plants and trees became more luxuriant. The fields of Sü Chou were of the middle first class, the revenues of the middle second class. Tribute was of the 'earths of five colors' (used in ceremonial architecture), variegated feathers of pheasants from the Yü valley, the solitary t'ung trees that grew on the southern slope of Mt. Yih and the musical stones that floated along the banks of the Si river. The Huai Yi barbarians brought oyster pearls and fish and baskets filled with black silk and fine-textured white silk."

In another ancient text (the *Chou Li*) the *ti-li* categorized the known natural regions into five "classes." The first region includes the mountains and forests, with species of fur-bearing animals and dark-colored plants; the people who live in this region are hairy and broad-shouldered. The second class of terrain includes the streams and lakes; there are fish and water plants. The people are dark-skinned and fat. In the third region, the hills and coast, there are winged creatures and fruit trees; the people are large. In the fourth region, which includes the river banks and low plains, there are shellfish and fruit plants and the people are slender. In the fifth class, in which are grouped the high plains and swamps, the animals are bare-skinned and the people are short and plump.

The *ti-li*, earth pattern, is a three-dimensional mosaic of land and people. It is not accidental that the description of each natural province ends with a comment on the "barbarians" who dwell within.

The conceptualization of landscape represented in these classical texts is cultural. Space is organized according to technology, and the perceived boundaries of space are culturally identified. Thus, for the lands of the cultivator we have detailed information about soil composition and the recognition of relevant ecological "markers" such as vegetation and animal species. Even the political model concedes the technological organization of space: while the west-east boundaries are fixed by desert and sea, the north-south regions—occupied by scarcely known peoples—are limitless.

CHAPTER IV

Artisan and Workshop

In the region of the present-day city of Chengchou, of northern Honan Province, Chinese archeologists have located and partially excavated about twenty-five settlements. These sites, first discovered in 1950, are scattered over an area of about forty square kilometers. They are the earliest concentration of a population which some call China's "oldest civilization." Sinologists have decided that the central ruins are of the "City of Ao," reported in early literary accounts to have been founded by Chung-ting, tenth king of the Shang dynasty, sometime in the fifteenth century B.C.

The central area of the City of Ao was roughly rectangular, 2 kilometers from north to south and 1.7 kilometers from east to west. It was surrounded by a wall of pounded earth. At one point the remains of the wall still stand four meters high, and it is twenty meters wide at the base. Ancient Chengchou was larger than the present-day city, but probably had a significance similar to its contemporary role: that of commanding an extremely important crossing of the Huangho. The city was located to the south of the river, on the banks of the Chinshui tributary, where the great alluvial plains of the east confront the rugged mountain escarpments of western Honan.

A perhaps irrelevant datum has been suggested by archeologist An Chih-huai: that it probably took ten thousand workers at least eighteen years to construct the wall, laboriously balancing on their shoulders the carrying poles laden with baskets of earth and then, with small wooden pounders, tamping the layers—some as thin as seven centimeters—each upon the lower within a wooden frame. Irrelevant because it is the wildest of guesses, but relevant because it gives us a hint as to the new vocabulary that must be used to describe the birth of a city, the meaning of urbanism and civilization. It is no longer appropriate to speak only of the daily drudgery of the peasant-farmer, soon to be called by the literati the "brown man," the man who had taken on the color of the earth and was baked by the sun. A new kind of person appeared on the historical stage, and it was the creation of his character that was the hallmark of the city. This was the craftsman, the artisan, who did not labor in the cultivated fields but in the mines and at forges, looms, and on earthworks.

Following the trajectory of time as the City of Ao came into being, it is best to approach the center from the periphery, for it is in the small nearby towns and the clusters of buildings on the outskirts of the wall that the first glimpse of the "new" man can be seen. He is alien and native, magician and scientist; and out of the essential interactions of these multi-ethnic, multi-linguistic communities were built the technocultural foundations of civilization. In the workshops around Chengchou, the skills and knowledge of the barbarian heritage complemented each other, stimulated and caused the efflorescence of a civilized style of life which we call "Shang."

The world-view of the artisan, that nature could be transformed by manual operations, was essentially a technological view that later was embodied in the literate tradition of Taoism:

> He who conforms to the course of the Tao, following the natural processes of Heaven and Earth, finds it easy to manage the whole world. Thus it was that Yü the Great was able to engineer the canals by following the nature of water and using it as his guide. Likewise Shen Nung: in the sowing of the seed, followed the nature of germination and thus obtained instruction. Waterplants root in water, trees in earth; birds fly in the air and beasts prowl on the ground; crocodiles and dragons live in the water, tigers and leopards dwell in mountains—such is their inherent nature. Pieces of wood when rubbed together generate heat, metal subjected to fire melts, wheels revolve, scooped out things float. All things have their natural tendencies.
>
> *Chuang Tzu*

It is fitting that we tour the environs of Chengchou, looking carefully into each of the shops to see the people at work, for there was a unity of techniques in the diverse crafts which developed during the Shang time which lent unity to the art style that came to be symbolic of the civilization. We cannot attempt to explain the iconography of this art style, since we are deprived of much of the contextual ideology, but we can explore its basis in the interdependence of techniques. In so doing we will have to cast aside the commonly held assumption that the artisan did not fully participate in the ideology; on the contrary, he gave it form.

As we move through the workshops of Chengchou, we will see clearly how the manufacturing methods of the Neolithic stoneworker and wood carver[1] were adapted to the

[1] For the moment, we must postpone talking of wood carving, for the art was apparently not practiced in shops and most probably remained an individual craft for a long time. It was plied at the sites of architectural construction, or in the coffin-chambers of the great tombs. We do not know where the wheelwrights worked, nor those who carved ceremonial vessels and musical instruments out of rare and costly woods.

media of bone and shell, how the metallurgist and potter used each other's products and wastes, how the potter learned about glazes from the slag left at the smiths' reducing hearth, how the smith got his crucibles from the potter.

THE BONE WORKSHOP

Near Ching Ching Shan, a settlement just north of the city wall, there was a workshop in which well over a thousand pieces of bone fragments of raw materials, half-finished artifacts, and the tools of manufacture were found. The materials were carefully selected—over 50 per cent were cut from splinters of human thigh bones, but there were also bones of pigs, oxen, deer, goats, and dogs. The same shop produced artifacts from elephant and boar tusks, deer antlers, and buffalo horns. (Where did the shop master get his rather macabre raw materials? Perhaps from neighboring people who exhumed and reburied their dead, perhaps from the remains of those who died as retainers of the aristocrats of the center city.) The workers sawed and roughly filed the bone pieces into blanks resembling the outline of the desired end product. They probably used saws and scrapers of stone. At first the workshops turned out only utilitarian objects: arrow points, handles for knives, awls, needles, fishhooks, and a few axe-heads. Then, for a period in late Shang times it became very fashionable to decorate the bone, and all objects were intricately carved. Many unfinished pieces bear the traces of paint used to sketch the designs before actually carving them with small knives of bronze and jade. The articles were then polished smooth with sandstone blocks.

The continuing elaboration of design is seen not so much in the tanged arrow points that were tied with soft leather thongs into socketed shafts, or even in the musical instruments—the barrel-shaped *hsuan* with a hole at the top for blowing into and five finger holes along the side to regulate pitch. It was the bone hairpins, so simple and small in the beginning, that changed with the times, becoming decorated in a style that is unmistakably Shang. At first the head of the pin became broad and flattened; sometimes it was carved with two openwork "legs" joined by a bridge. By late Shang times, the head of the hairpin was considered as an object in itself and was even detachable from the socketed shaft. It was carved into outline shapes of birds and animals (sometimes even a human figure appears) and then designs were meticulously engraved over the entire surface. Sometimes the carvings were inlaid with small fragments of shell or stone. Larger pieces of shell, imported from the Yangtze Valley, were treated much like bone, often carved into plaques that were strung together as a form of breastplate "armor." Ivory staff heads and long bone handles and containers were also entirely covered with exquisite designs as the craftsman gained greater control of the materials and exulted in his skills.

POTTERY WORKSHOP

About 1200 meters west of the wall of Chengchou, in an area of about 4000 square meters, there were fourteen pottery kilns. These were located quite near to the river banks; the Chinshui clays may have been a source of the potters raw material. In addition to the kilns, there were pits filled with unfired vessels, broken bits of pottery and the refuse of the kilnmaster's mistakes: the warped, cracked, and misfired pottery. There were the tools of the trade: pottery anvils and carved clay stamps, and there also the houses of the kiln workers.

Previously we have discussed pottery as a cultural artifact, for its intrinsic potential in permitting us to glimpse the value system of its makers and users some five thousand years ago. In describing Chengchou and the emerging civilization of the first millennium B.C. it is possible to learn even more about the sociology and ideology of the people by treating not the pottery—but the techniques of manufacture—as cultural artifacts. For it is here that we confront the need for a new vocabulary, occasioned by new economic relationships and technological interdependence. The workshop symbolizes the emergence of the peasantry in a real sense: the craftsman produces too much for elite consumption alone, he produces within a system of redistribution that eventually breaks the Neolithic self-sufficiency of the village and ties the peasant to the market, thus making him a participant in the formulation of a civilizational style.

There were few technical improvements in the manufacturing of pottery in Chengchou, although those that did come were largely borrowed from the neighboring metallurgist. The significant changes were in the form of new social arrangements of production which made it feasible to increase capital equipment and produce in quantity. Assuming that the social structure of any manufacturing organization is partly determined by the technical processes involved and partly by the system of redistribution, let us examine the ceramic industry as we know it archeologically at Chengchou.

The steps in the making of pottery are not many, although the text of the *Chou Li* comments that earth is one of the classes of "worked" materials which requires only two "operations." The primary necessity is of course the collection of raw materials. Although in many areas of the world there must be tedious and often hazardous expeditions to the source of available clays, it is more common to find that the sites of manufacture are located where clay and fuel are available in quantity. (Most of the clays found in the ancient pottery of Northern China are loessic, proving local derivation.) This explains the pattern of concentration of potters' settlements around Chengchou and elsewhere. Whether these neighborhoods or little villages were formed into caste-like organizations we cannot say, but certainly the closeness of the families and the similarities of daily routine fostered the kinds of standardization that workshop production demanded of the artisans. Although women may have gathered the clay from the stream beds and levigated it, washing out impurities, the potters were most certainly men.

The second major technical step involves creation of the vessel. Although standardization was now the rule (the texts of a few hundreds of years later describe in precise detail the specifications of the named vessels) and tradition and function narrowly dictated the shape, each pot evolved from the potter's hands as a new creation.

The fast turning wheel was not much used in Shang pottery-making, largely because it presented mechanical problems that required more experimentation with advanced rotary motion utilizing metal bearings. All pottery was made by three basic techniques, frequently combined as the potter attempted to cope with the problems of shaping wet clay that tended to collapse and then shrink and crack as it dried. The potter did not necessarily rationalize these processes, but may have experienced them as unanalyzed relationships dependent upon the properties of the materials he was using. The mistakes were easy to name: the uneven thickness of the walls, the misshapen rim, etc.

Small pots were made by ring, or coil, building, although often a small bowl would be molded by pressing the wet clay into a previously fired bowl or a carved block of wood. Larger bowls and jars were frequently made in two sections, then linked together with wet clay after they had partially dried. This was done because the pots might sag under their own weight, although sometimes they were bound up with string. In order to disguise the join, the potter devised a sharply carinated (keeled) shoulder, frequently mistaken as an imitation of metal forms.

Both of these techniques, inherited from the village potter

who preceded him, were employed by the Shang craftsmen, but more important in his repertoire—and a significant link in the inter-locked technologies of ceramics and bronze casting—were the use of the belt-mold and of the paddle and anvil. The belt-mold, also a traditional technique, was used especially in building up the walls of large, deep cooking vessels. A curved strip of wood (or bamboo) of about two inches in diameter, wrapped round with string or cord, was pressed against strips or coils of clay, adding successively to the height of the vessel. As the belt-mold was pulled away (the string would act as an anti-adhesive), the potter would smooth the clay with his wettened hand, often obliterating the vertical string markings. The rims of these vessels were fashioned by hand.

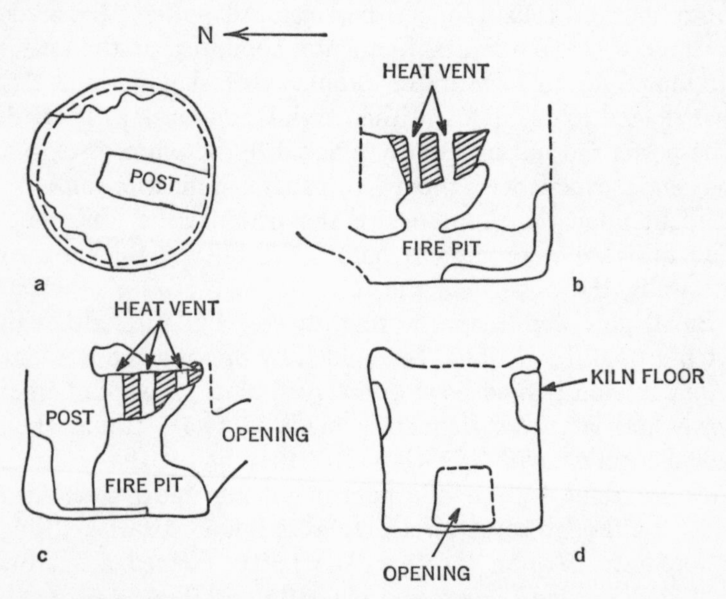

Fig. 8 Early Shang pottery kiln, Lo Ta Miao
(a) Plan at base (b) Plan at the opening on top (c) Cross-section at AA′ (d) Cross-section at BB′

Allied to this technique of forming the body of a vessel was the use of a rounded pottery anvil, which was held inside the pot while the artisan slowly spun the turntable on which the wet clay rested. As the pot turned, he beat on the outside of the walls with a wooden paddle, gradually thinning and building it up to the desired height. Sometimes the paddle was wrapped with string or matting, and sometimes it was carved with simple designs. In its turn, the carved paddle developed into the clay medallion that was used to stamp complex designs not only on fine pottery, but on the molds used in bronze casting as well. And, at least by late Shang times, complex piece molds were being used to construct the bulbous hollow legs of the li tripod.

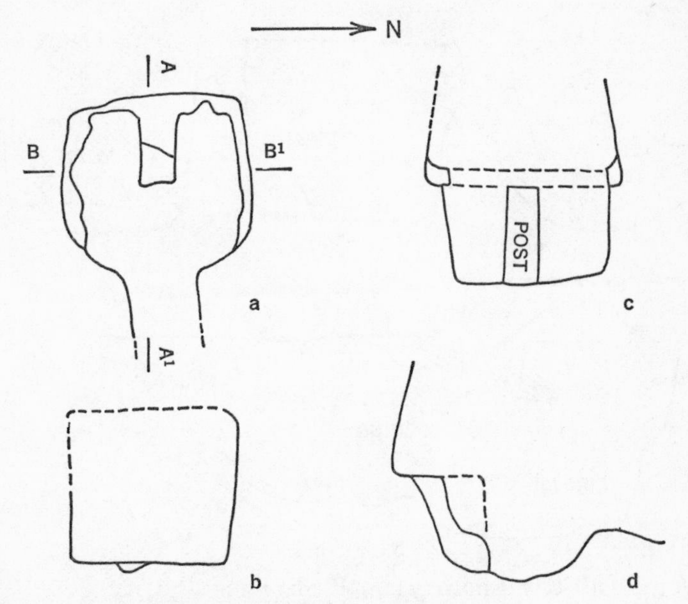

Fig. 9 Middle Shang pottery kiln, Ming Kung Lu
(a) Plan at the base (b) Cross-section of the base from the east (c) Cross-section of the base from the west (d) Cross-section of the base from the north

Until this point in the process, the act of production has been in the potter's hands—and in his mind, for always there must be a preconcept of the finished vessel and always there is the seriousness with which the artist transforms consciousness into object.

The next major step is pyrotechnical. That it embodied the merging of mysticism with science is well illustrated by the legends of heroic master potters who threw themselves into the kiln so as to have a more perfect firing; who, once wafted away in smoke, became immortal.

Although the aesthetically appreciated qualities of color

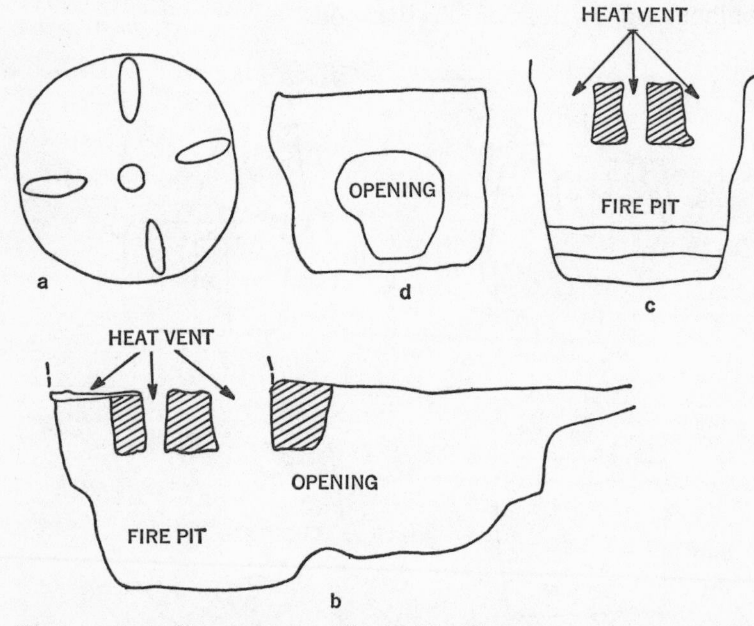

Fig. 10 Late Shang pottery kiln, Pi Sha Kang
(a) Plan of the baking floor (b) Cross-section of the fire pit at the opening (c) Cross-section of the fire pit at the side (d) Front view at the opening of the fire pit

result from the differential firing of clay (as well as from the intrinsic mineral content), the purpose of firing is to render the pot durable and reduce its porosity so that it may serve its primary function as a container. Kiln firing, which began very early in the Neolithic of China, is superior to the open-firing of pots because higher temperatures can be achieved and the kilnmaster has more control of the atmosphere surrounding the pots. However, where the open pit could be stoked with brush and dung, the enclosed kiln required billets of wood or charcoal; therefore the governing element in the location of a kiln may well have been its nearness to forest-land. In China, the only kind of kiln used prior to modern times was the vertical kiln, which essentially is a cylinder that encloses hot gases emitted from the hearth at its base and leads them upwards towards a dome where the gases escape through an opening. In its simplest form, the dome was temporary, composed merely of layers of potsherds resting on the pots being fired—but even this detail indicates the quantity of pottery that was manufactured. If we recall the kilns of Pan P'o village, they were already of the permanent type, with kiln chambers removed from the fire passages by narrowed earthen walls. The problem of protecting the pots from contact with the flames was solved at the Chengchou kilns in a number of ways. The earliest of the kilns incorporated a perforated clay shelf about eighteen inches above the floor. The hot gases rose through the perforations and were deflected by the domed roof. Since this was a permanent construction, there was a stoke-hole in the side of the kiln to maintain the fire. The difficulty of supporting the shelf meant that the diameter of the kiln shaft was restricted, in this case to about four feet.

At the Lo Ta Miao site (called "proto-Shang") some improvement had been made in supporting the shelf of the chamber by having a rectangular wooden post project from the western wall of the kiln. The inner walls, still quite small in size, were plastered with a layer of straw-tempered clay that turned green and very hard from the fire. The kiln builders at Ming Kung-lu attempted several solutions to the problem of regulating the draught and thus controlling the atmosphere in the firing chamber. The expenditure of such ingenuity is an index of the demand for true standardization of production.

The innovations made by these Shang kilnmasters approached those found in the horizontal kilns of later times. The vents were arranged in the firing-chamber floor so that the gases would rise evenly into the chamber and then out through baked clay chimneys. The newly developed kilns were able to produce temperatures sufficiently high to make stoneware (with a fairly regular hardness of five) which had a thin, pale yellowish-green glaze applied to the outside and sometimes the interior of the pots.

In part this experimentation with the technical process of firing was with color, but this must have been a minor feature. Less and less of the redwares and blackwares were made, while a more uniform greyware, possibly produced by an imbibing process of adding wet grass to the kiln as it began to cool, came to dominate the industry.

A certain specialization of product became associated with particular kilns, some making the culinary ware—grey pottery which included great quantities of sand temper to prevent cracking during repeated heating over cooking fires—some the finer pottery, some the stoneware, and others the white kaolin ware that was probably used exclusively by the wealthy, as ritual ware and for display.

BRONZE WORKSHOPS

Outside the ancient wall of Ao there were two widely separated areas in which bronze workers lived and worked. Here were the foundries, the slag, the floors layered with the remains of once molten copper now oxidized by time. Here the broken clay crucibles and pouring beakers, a thousand fragments of earthenware molds and clay cores, and the small bronze objects of everyday use—the knives, arrowheads, and fishhooks; and again, here also the homes of the workers. It may well be that the numerous families were organized into "forges" as in other parts of the preindustrial world; if so, the range of specialized skills within the social unit would have been very large indeed.

These are the earliest foundries as yet known from excavations in China. The simplest of two-part molds were used. A slab of baked clay into which a half-dozen arrowhead shapes were hollowed, each connected to a central channel "like the veins of a leaf," and over which a second slab, hollowed so as to match, was placed and bound with cord. The molten metal was poured into the mold. After cooling, the arrowheads were cut off the central stem. A slightly more complex mold was used for making a socketed axe-head: a clay core, provided with lugs for fitting it into a mold with a pouring vent at the top.

The acquisition of empirical knowledge that brought the barbarian heritage to the threshold of civilization is fully exposed in the metallurgical revolution that brought these workshops into being. Once again we must slow down and search out patiently the technical steps that lead to the manufactured product, remembering that these "techniques" are the expression of cultural, cognitive, and social behavior.

Bronze is an alloy of copper and tin, frequently found with small amounts of other elements, such as lead, zinc, and occasionally silver. The largest copper deposits in China are in Yunnan, Szechwan, and Hsikang, but there is also some copper in the northern provinces. There is also a relatively wide distribution of copper in Shensi and Honan. Almost all of the copper used in the bronzes of this early period were of "secondary" ore formation, which means that they were either the oxides (cuprite and temorite) or carbonates (malachite, azurite). These are found near the ground surface, where they are acted upon by air and water, resulting in bright and easily recognizable earth colors of red and green. Tin is not so readily found, occurring mostly in Yunnan and elsewhere in the south, although it has been claimed that stream-tin did formerly exist amongst the gravels of rivers in the vicinity of the late Shang city of Anyang.

The ancient "miners" did not require special equipment for their task, but a finely developed lore of topography and mineralogy. In the earliest of texts there is the recognition of "earths of many colors," the veneration of mountains and rocks of awesome shape and the streams with floating stones!

The first step of transformation of the raw materials is the smelting. This is the process that is filled with mystery—and fear—for the uninitiated. The chemical reaction occurs under combustion, the crushed ores are mixed with carbon (such as charcoal) so that the oxygen, sulphur, and other nonmetallic elements escape, leaving the molten metal free. In the Chengchou workshops, the smelting was done at first in conical basins dug into the floor. Later crucibles may have been used, and eventually furnaces that imitated the pottery kilns. The copper and tin were probably smelted together. Tin increased the liquidity of the melt and made casting easier. Later on tin was smelted at its source of origin and transported to the factories in ingots. Lead, which may at first have been accidentally introduced into the alloy, soon became valued for its own properties: casting of vessels in lead was sometimes done to duplicate the more costly bronze, but it also was added to the copper and tin to lower the melting point and make the finished product easier to polish and brighten. Sometimes up to 20 per cent of a bronze alloy was composed of lead.

Passages in the *Chou Li* and the *Shih Chi* have been interpreted to report specific formulae for the composition of the alloys to be used in the manufacture of different classes of artifacts. Thus, bells and *ting* cauldrons were to be six parts copper and one of tin, hatchets and axes five parts of copper to one part of tin, daggers four parts of copper to one part tin, swords were to be 3:1, little arrows and knives 5:2, while the alloys for mirrors were to be made of equal parts.

The complete and significant gap between technologist and intelligentsia-literati had begun, forever to plague the development of science in China! There are no regularities in the alloys, neither in the major components nor in the impurities found mixed in with the ores. The most common impurity (apart from lead) is iron, which may have come from the clays of the crucible itself. Silver and gold, occurring in amounts of up to 0.1 per cent of the alloy, occur naturally with copper and tin; the only significant relationship in the composition of the alloy comes when zinc and possibly

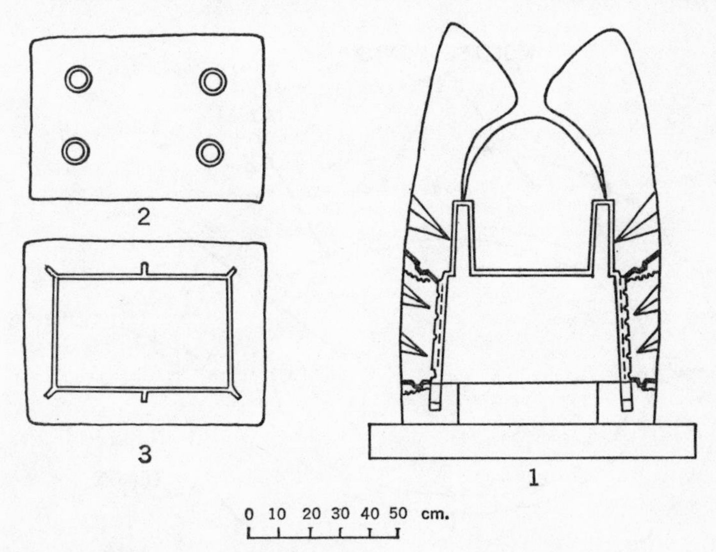

Fig. 11 Mold-casting of Bronzes
(1) Cross-section of the mold (2) Cross-section at the legs
(3) Cross-section at the body of the vessel

phosphorous are added, but this did not happen until the Han period.

The texts were slightly more accurate when they observed:

> In preparing the molten substance to pour into a mold, the metal [copper] is combined with the tin and a black vapor is given off. The vapor then turns yellowish-white and then it is dissipated. Blue-white vapor appears and is succeeded by pure blue: then the metal is ready for pouring.

As soon as the output of bronze increased in significant quantity, it is fairly certain that the ores were refined, at least in part, at the source. The economy in transport also meant a further social specialization of craft that in turn led to innovations in furnace types and the probably early invention of the piston-bellows. But this latter is a little ahead of the story. At the foundries of Chengchou the smelting and casting were functionally unified, and at the same time de-

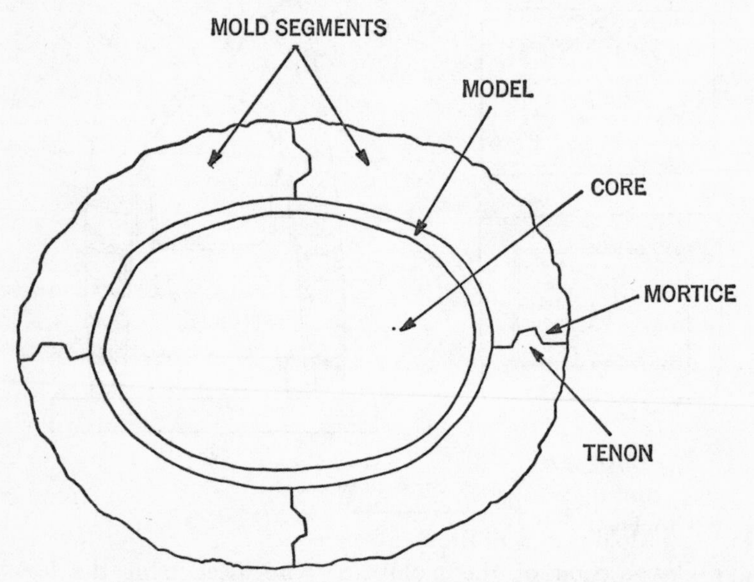

Fig. 12 Cross-section of a piece mold assembly

pendent upon innovations being made in the ceramic workshops.

There were several varieties of crucibles in use, basically directed at retaining the maximum heat within the vessel so that the metal could remain in a molten state until the moment of pouring. The most interesting was the double-walled crucible, the interstices of which were filled with sand and fibrous materials that were non-conductors of heat. At the time this kind of crucible was in use it is certain that the refining of ores was no longer being done in the foundry, and only the alloys were melted in the crucible.

Although the moment of pour must have been one of great tension throughout the shop, there was confidence also, founded on the mold-making technique that had been co-developed by the potter and the bronze caster. The casting of an object is simply the making of a replica in bronze of a model created in another medium. In ancient China, the medium was clay.

Ironically, it has taken the most sophisticated and complex of modern analytical technology, plus verification by replication in contemporary laboratories, to understand how the early craftsmen executed their work. To make the undecorated vessels, the model of clay (most frequently a familiar pottery form) was shaped and baked around a clay core. Slabs of fresh clay were fitted against the model and, after having received the imprint, were removed in segments. The number of segments depended upon the shape and design of the vessel. The model was then scraped away from the core, the mold segments reassembled and held together by a mortice and tenon construction. Before reassembling the mold, small rectangular chaplets made of scraps of bronze were inserted to ensure proper alignment of the segments and to keep the space between the core and mold constant. The mold, a product of ceramic technology, was ready to receive the molten alloyed metal. The specially prepared crucibles kept the molten bronze at a very high temperature to avoid too sudden cooling on contact with the mold. In casting larger vessels, sprues, or ducts, were provided to conduct the molten bronze into the mold cavity, but when casting tripod vessels, the legs themselves were frequently used as sprues.

We can see the technology of the bronze worker take over completely from the ceramic specialist when we recognize that he frequently shaped the core to leave depressions that would compensate for shrinkage of the metal after cooling, and even more starkly when we view the skill with which foundry accidents were corrected. Not only are there clever patches and mends, but one remarkable example has been found where an entire leg, which failed to form in the first cast, was replaced.

By the time of the late complex of settlements and tombs of Yin at Anyang, when incredibly large vessels were being cast, the technique of pouring itself became a craft. Again, specialization and innovation coincided as new problems inherent in the process were attacked and solved. To cast the famous Ssu Mu Hu *ting*, which weighs over one ton, pouring channels were fashioned which brought the molten bronze directly from the furnace area to the mold inlet. The furnace was an open trench of over eight meters in length, and one can easily picture the sweating workers shovelling, stoking, and operating leather bellows day and night to achieve and maintain the heat necessary for the melt! Again, large-scale industrial production is signalled in the Chou period, when earthern cores were used for the separate firing of handles and legs, and these members were then inserted into suitable openings in the piece-mold of the body so that when the metal was poured to form the vessel the appendages were joined to it.

One final comment concerning the piece-mold technique—although the segments could have been reused, they were not;

no replication of vessels has been found, so that each complete object reflects the aesthetic conceptualization and choices of the craftsman. And yet, as we shall see, both the content and the structure of these choices were technical solutions to technical problems inherent in the casting process itself.

The artistic appreciation expressed by our contemporary viewing of ancient Chinese bronzes, the wonder and excitement are derived from the rhythmic repetition of pattern, the interplay of low and high relief, the ever-so-fine control of the savage and wild imagery, and the bizarre shapes of the vessels themselves. These very features are the ones that emerge from the nature of the craft. They were not dictated from some external elite to uncomprehending laborers, but were formulated by the artisans into a common iconography.

There are only a few known decorated bronze vessels that come from the Chengchou workshops, and these are thin-walled and of simple décor that runs in horizontal zones. The artisan first prepared a clay model of the vessel shape and pressed the segmented piece-mold against it to record this shape. He then cut a negative impression of the design into the segments, so that after the pouring the décor appeared in relief. This is an almost total borrowing of ceramic technology, if we recall the manufacture of the belt-molded pottery. The joins between the segments of the mold are visible on the finished bronze.

At first, leakage of metal at the joins was cleverly worked into flanges running along the edges of the vessel, although in some highly finished pieces of later times they were filed until invisible. At the other extreme, the flanges themselves became surfaces upon which to execute decorative imagination. The significant point, however, is that the arrangement of décor on the vessel came to be dependent on the use of sectional molds.

The décor which one sees on the finished bronze object is the result of a transference of a positive representation made on the model in relief to a negative in the mold, and then back to the positive in the cast bronze. The only other possibility of achieving relief on the cast bronze was by carving negatively into the mold itself. The Neolithic potter had already demonstrated appreciation of the value of negative motif in painting. Its utilization in mold manufacture brought the concept to maturity in the hands of the metallurgist; both the model and the mold came to be seen not as pottery but as part of the process of casting. Most commonly, deep relief designs were carved in the model, while low relief was incised—or stamped—into the mold. Generally, the *lei-wen* designs, thunder and lightning (spiral and key), that fill the spaces of the surface of each vessel, running in and around the main figures, are in low relief, contrasting with the bold surfaces of the animal, bird, and human figures.

One cannot rightfully "explain" the meaning of the *lei-wen* pattern, or the artistic desire to so completely fill space, but how the finished vessel must have glistened and shone: the fine-lined designs reflecting light and shadow in a moiré pattern that imparted motion and depth to the vision!

However, the piece-mold design also dictated the ultimate design; not only did flanges delineate the join of segments, they came to determine the rhythms of the decoration, the horizontal zones of patterning, and the repetition of design features. Wilma Fairbanks (1962:14) has suggested that the sectionalism of piece-mold assemblage was in part "cause" of the reknowned *t'ao t'ieh* figure: the mask of the dragon, or "Great Glutton." She explains the split image as it appears on the bronze as the result of using segments containing mirror-images of each half of the mask. This reversal is repeated segment by segment around the circumference of the vessel, and the evidence is in the great "eyes" of the monster; in reality the eyes are an artistic device of disguising the raised bosses that were sculpted onto the clay model so as to maintain space between model and mold during the pouring:

> Each boss in a segment was paired with the boss in an adjoining segment—in the mind of the designer—and regarded as a pair of eyes. To add the paired horns, ears, nostrils, jaws, etc., for a monster mask was but a matter of transferring to the ceramic bronze pattern features which had presumably been developed in various carving media. Since the eyes were paired equidistant from the mold-join it was logical for the entire design to develop symmetrically and the pattern of one segment to be the mirror-image of its neighbor.

The significance of sectionalism is twofold—the first so obvious in the technical relationship of art and medium. The second is sociological, in that the workshop took on one further aspect of specialization of skill, and probably of manpower. The artisan had at his disposal "dies" which he could manipulate and combine according to his own devising but of course with symbolic meaningfulness. How close we are to the invention of printing, how close to the use of formalized ideographic writing. Did every workshop-foundry have workers capable of engraving inscriptions on clay blocks that were pressed into slabs to be incorporated into the prepared vessel mold?

JADE WORKING

Of the remaining classes of "worked" materials, jade and leather and fibres, we have as yet no archeological locations of workshops, but must rely on inferential evidence alone. Dependent in many ways—technical and stylistic—on the bronze workshop, jade commanded the attention of very early writers for its intrinsic qualities:

> Jade is a stone that is beautiful. It has five virtues: there is warmth in its lustre and brilliance, this is the manner of kind-

ness; its soft interior may be viewed from outside revealing the goodness within, this is the manner of rectitude; its note is tranquil and high, and carries far and wide, this is the way of wisdom; it may be broken but cannot be twisted, this is the manner of bravery; its sharp edges are not intended for violence, this is the way of purity. (Translation after Ching, *Shang China*, 1960:109.)

Jade commands our respect and admiration, for not only is it rare and extremely difficult to work as a medium of artistic expression (the very term has taken on the meaning of *virtue*), but it was used in the Shang tradition to capture in miniature the style that was developed towards monumentality in bronze. All "jade" worked in China before the eighteenth century A.D. was nephrite, a silicate of calcium and magnesium with a hardness of 6½ and a refractive index of 1.6. Nephrite, the "plummage of the kingfisher" was found in the Ho T'ien region of Khotan and in Central Asia. There are early paintings of women fording the streams, searching for the precious jade pebbles. As noted previously, nephrite was also worked natively in the Lake Baikal region of Siberia. Many softer materials, especially limestone, were frequently used to imitate or substitute for jade in making the large vessels that were fashionable for a time.

The working of jade is not sculpture, since it is too hard to be chiseled and flaked. It must be ground and polished by abrasive sands carried in a moist or oily medium—once again, a technique carried through the centuries and reinterpreted in a very different context. No marks are made upon the jade by the bamboo, wood, or metal tools that carry the abrasive. It is assumed that quartz sand was used at first and then crushed almandine garnets and eventually corundum. Bamboo was used extensively to drill through the circular bracelets and *pi* of Neolithic times. When bronze tools were used, a new technique developed.

Both sides of a cut slab of jade were incised with a knife.

The incising was deep and the edges of the incision were bevelled and rounded to give the impression of a multi-dimensional object. More and more, the stone was treated with natural rounded surfaces; sometimes pairs of parallel lines would be incised and bevelled, or even inclined planes would be ground between the incisions, leaving the areas in thread-relief. Imagine the tiniest of cicadas, folded wings lined with every vein, the elegant man, standing two inches high—each detail of clothing clearly to be seen!

Sawing of the slabs of jade that were to be carved was probably done with flat straight-edged hand saws of slate. There are early examples of discs in which a straight groove or ridge shows where the saw cuts were made from either end but failed to meet. The only rotary tool was the bamboo drill fitted with a point of bronze and turned with a pump-bow. Indeed, jade working was probably a craft practiced in the home by specially talented men until the foundries and markets were able to produce iron tools. Then the ease of carving and acceleration of production may have been facilitated by drawing these artisans together in shops, although production was still limited by the supply of raw materials.

One gets this impression from the diversity of jade objects that were produced after iron tools are introduced; many of the open-worked plaques and "pendants" meant to be sewn onto cloth or leather garments are not nearly as refined as the earlier jades, and frequently use serpentine rather than nephrite.

Because jades are generally considered as objects of art, items embodying status and luxury, there is difficulty in interpreting them from the distance of fifteen centuries. This difficulty is in part inherent in the legacy of sinology, the use of ancient textual information that is a ". . . chimera based on a commentator's interpretation of a ritualist's conception of the role played by a given jade, known to him, in a ritual that may never have been enacted." Another approach, which does not destroy our aesthetic appreciation and respect for the craftsmanship of the lapidary, but indeed enhances it, is the study of certain jades as elements in technology. The significance of this interpretation lies in proving, once again, that the division between technology, science, and ideology was non-existent in early China, but came after the true stratification of the political state.

In the *Shu Ching* there is a passage in which it is said that the "Emperor Shun examined the *hsun chi yü hêng* in order to regulate the Seven Directors." The Seven Directors have variously been interpreted as the sun, moon, and five planets, or as Ursa Major. The *hsun chi yü hêng* has been translated as a gem-adorned turning sphere and jade transverse (tube). In the literate cosmology of China these two objects took on the symbology of heaven and earth.

It has recently been pointed out that during the first millennium B.C., when most large constructions in ancient China were apparently oriented towards the north, the north star itself was not clearly visible. A means of determining true north would have been required. It has been suggested that the *hsun chi*, a serrated-jade disc, was in fact a stellar template, calibrated so that if the notches along the perimeter were superimposed on the "Directors"—the stars of the Great Dipper, the central hole of the disc would be centered on true north. To fix the position of north by this means, the observer would have required a sighting tube. This was the *yü hêng*, the jade transverse, which has been shown to fit into the discs. On nearly every disc there are two series of incised lines, one, a double line, is tangent to the central hole, the second is perpendicular to the first and diametral. If the leading edge of the squared sighting tube were aligned with the double line, the nocturnal rotation of the circumpolar stars could be calculated. Thus the instrument was used as a "star dial," a means of recording time by night. Alignment with the diametral line may have been an aid predicting the solstices.

If the interpretation is correct, this is an extraordinary example of a technological invention preceding the development of a ritualized symbology, but it also underscores the essential interplay of knowledge between the technician-artisan and the scientist.

LEATHER WORKING

Once again we must rely upon textual information (and, in this case, ethnographic example) to reconstruct the technology of the leather worker's craft. The *Chou Li* says that skin working, which took five manual-chemical operations, included the making of armor and drums and the preparation of leather and fur garments. "The cuirasse which is made of the skin of wild cattle sewn in seven [layers] will last 100 years."

Various chemical arts were involved in the preparation of hides in the early Han period, and we may safely assume a much earlier practice of this craft. The first step, when preparing the heavy calf and cattle hides, was to soften them in pits built of stone and as deep as six feet into the ground. Sometimes salt was added to the water, making a briny solution. The hides were then stretched over wooden beams and scraped clean of impurities with a blunt stone knife. A paste of lime and water was diluted into a "milk" which was put into a brick pit of great depth. The hides were put into this lime pit, and it was covered over with a reed or bamboo matting. After ten days, the hides were removed and worked with a blunt knife until all the hair was removed and a two-handled sharp knife was used to clean the hide of flesh and fat. The hide was then smoked over a large semi-subterranean rectangular stove built of mud-brick and fueled with straw. It was constantly sprinkled with water. After smoking, the skins were spread on the ground and covered with sodium sulphate. After thirty to forty minutes they were smoked again. This process was repeated three or four times. Finally the hide was softened by scraping it with a brick.

If a soft, fine white leather was to be made from sheepskin, it was worked with a semi-lunar knife and then delimed by rubbing it with chicken dung. After tanning with the sodium sulphate it was washed and dried in the air on a wooden frame.

SILK WEAVING

The early history of silk weaving is as yet unknown. There were no traces of this craft at Chengchou, but several remarkable discoveries in the later Shang tombs at Anyang suggest that textile production may in part have been removed from the household. The technical complexity of the fragments found encrusted in the bronzes buried in these tombs could only have been woven on the many-heddled looms that one would expect to find in a shop but not a small house. Early textual references to "Supervisors of Weaving" support this idea. On the other hand, the raising and feeding of silkworms and the infinitely laborious task of reeling the thread from the steamed cocoons were probably done by women and children in the great concentration of labor that these seasonal tasks require.

The fact that the silken thread—sometimes over a thousand meters emerging from one cocoon—retains its original viscous coating, and was not spun, shows an appreciation for the extraordinary tensile strength of silk and also gives a special character to early Shang silk weaving.

In all Shang examples that have been discovered, the looms that produced them were threaded so that either warp and weft were equal in count, or the warp was slightly denser. Some weaving was so coarse as to appear gauze-like, while one specimen of tabby has a very fine rep of seventy-two warp threads and thirty-five weft threads in each square centimeter.

One of the most interesting features of the silks is the presence of a twill weave as well as plain weaving, and the use of embroidery. There is also one specimen of a silk mosaic, three pieces of fabric cut and sewn together into a design. There is no other indication of dyeing, but some of the threads appear to have been washed—which may mean that color was applied afterwards.

The extraordinary value placed on silk, appreciation of the complexity of its production, and possibly its very early role as a tribute-unifier of far-flung ethnic groupings were expressed by the use to which the Shang silks were put: they were wrapped with care and delicacy around the precious bronze vessels and ceremonial weapons that were placed with the dead. Who were the men that commanded this expression of wealth and possibly chiefly status?

Before attempting to answer this question, let us stop a moment; the tour is over, there are no more shops to look into. We cannot peer over the wall into the inner city of Chengchou because it remains unexcavated—it still lives.

The workshops and the technology of the crafts were presented in great detail, or at least in the greatest detail possible through archeological reconstruction. Why have we dwelt on these processes and techniques? The first answer is that the history of technology demands it—and must remain dissatisfied with our uneven evidence. The anthropologist looks to the detail itself. How else can the embroidery of our imaginations take on the color and richness of life in prehistory? We cannot re-create the slap of hands on wet clay, the songs of the women searching for precious stones in the streams, the heat of the kiln, or the rhythm of the bellows. Nor can we re-create the mystery of alchemy, the prayers and chants that accompanied the mixing of metals in the crucible, the sleepless nights that preceded the warping of the loom, or the visions of design that filled the dreams of the bronze caster. Thus we must be content with noting the richness of detail that we can recognize in the technological processes. We can appreciate the complexity of human skill and knowledge, and it is in these that we look for the beginnings of "civilization."

It was from the workshops that the romanticized descriptions of the *Yü Kung* took their meaning. It was to the workshops that the "foreigners" brought baskets heaped with varnish and lead, hemp and pearls, the fruit of the pine, the many-colored silks, the floss, the purple dyes, the cinnabar, the feathers of wild fowl, the bamboo, the reeds and the grass cloth, the hides and furs, the cedar, camphor, and cypress woods, the jade, the flint and the salt, the corundum, tin, iron and steel. And the people that brought these things were fat and slender, tall and short, brown and yellow, hairy and hairless. With the laden baskets they brought also knowledge of the raw materials of the natural world and the skills and techniques with which to transform them.

A cultural unity began to grow out of the workshops, in part perhaps a result of the need to communicate these experiences and techniques, to teach the succeeding generations and to innovate. We will never know the ritual and drama, the legends and invocations, dancing, fasting, and feasting that accompanied each process of material transformation; the lore that embodied the unanalyzed but empirically experienced techniques.

The only aspect of this unity that we can regard is the interdependence of techniques already described: the recognition of the transformation of elements through the application of heat, the pyrotechnic control of kiln and furnace, the concept of replicating shapes by using molds, and the related idea of interchangeability of design elements by using stamps or dies. Some industries could not, by the nature of their materials, be affected by these techniques. Yet both jade and silk were brought into the tradition through a transference of art motifs.

Something else was happening on the outskirts of the wall, and this was the increasing outward circulation of specialized goods, many bearing the hallmarks of the emerging civilization. The Neolithic mosaic as we previously pictured it was able to absorb the excitement of this style, to modify and to interpret it in many differing ways. This was not yet the time of the urban revolution; preceding the true demographic features of urbanism, a network of specialized access, exploitation, and distribution of resources and wealth was working itself out.

The period we mistakenly call "Shang" represents a curious moment in time—a moment at the threshold of crystallization of the stratified state. This is most clearly seen in the inscriptions found on the bronzes: they do not tell of virtuous deeds and munificent rewards, they all follow a simple formula, designed to reinforce the continuity of lineage, the "charter" of status. The inscriptions begin with the name of the person making (paying for) the vessel, followed by the name of the ancestor for whom it has been made. This is followed by the ancestor's honorific title, usually preceded by *fu*, father, and a date. The inscription ends with the designation of the vessel type and the admonition "it is to be preserved."

The mistake in labelling this period "Shang" is that we shall see similar developments in many parts of the country we call China, although it is only for Shang that we have a written literature in the form of the succeeding dynastic histories.

CHAPTER V

Styles

We will not label this period of 1500–700 B.C. in ontological terms; it is not a moment of birth, for civilizations are not born. They, as individual human beings, develop a consciousness, an arrangement of cultural symbols that encodes and defines the "style" or meaning of life that can be identified by the outsider. By 700 B.C. almost two hundred ethnic units were recognized by the administrators of the emerging Chou state. These were not simple contending rivals; many of them were undergoing metamorphosis as they were involved in an increasing interaction of trade and commerce. It was in part out of this economic interaction that the political order became formalized in late Chou times.

We see this process *in embryo* when reading the oracles written by Shang diviners. During the ascendancy of the chief Wu Ting the names of over thirty tribes are mentioned, people who lived beyond the Shang "borders," in Shansi and Shensi across the T'ai Hang range. According to the inscriptions, "military campaigns" were led against these people. The tribal labels are not consistent, they shift and fade; after the period when the Shang dominated the Huang plain, many of the names disappear. According to traditional history, the people were absorbed and assimilated into the Chinese grand

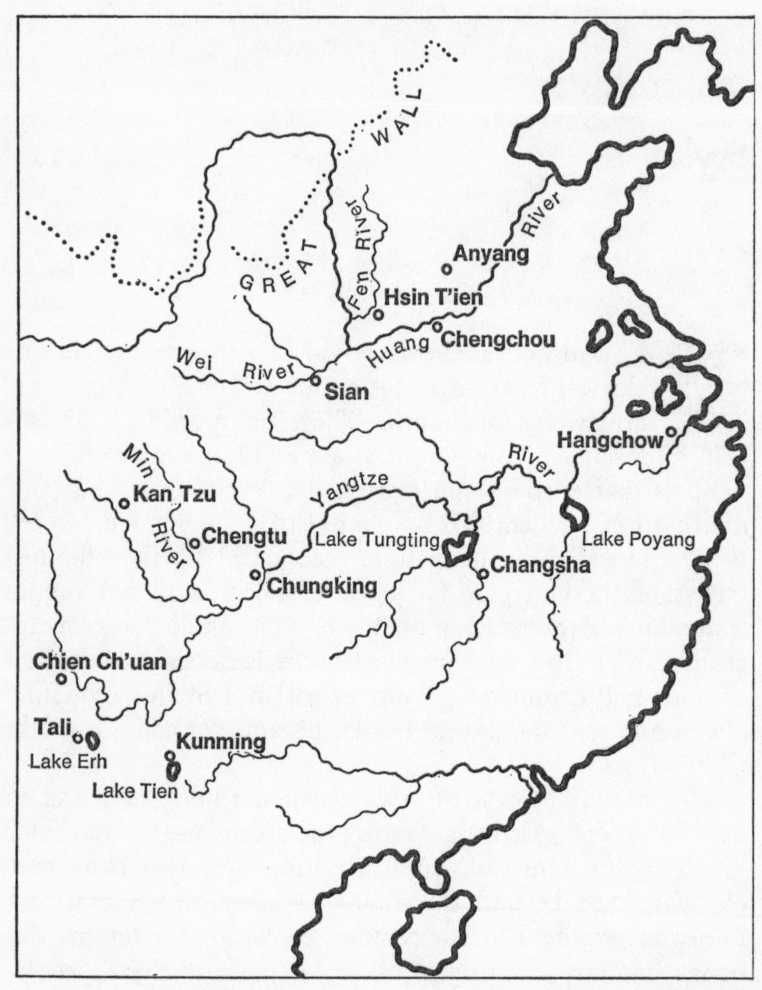

Fig. 13 Geographical setting of sites mentioned in Chapters V and VI

style. In reality, the territorial interstices between all the budding states continued to be filled with the shifting, nameless cultural units. In the case of Shang-Chou emergence, the struggle for self-identification was resolved through a growing administrated trade, as the center came to terms with the "barbarians," the outsiders, creating a system of tribute and commerce that required managerial controls and regularized borders.

The first step of this emergence was the elaboration of a ceremonial system that gave legitimacy to certain lineages and that established the stratified statuses of the other social and ethnic groups with whom these lineages were to interact. We will shortly see how the pattern of "warfare" in Shang and early Chou was not to gain territory, not to enslave populations, but to capture the sacrificial victims necessary for these self-reinforcing rituals. Gradually, these ceremonials were eliminated as the administrative mode became dominant, as it ensured access to the sources of needed raw materials and transportation of these and refined products.

In the southwest of China, the mode that facilitated the crystallization of political identity was a far-flung commerce that grew out of special access to primary resources and trade routes and consequently resulted in the uneven distribution of wealth. A social hierarchy, technologically supported by intensified agriculture, developed on this basis. However, in contrast to the north, which turned ever in on itself, the southwest was able to maintain constantly open channels of cultural communication while the variegated topographical map continued to correspond to a contemporary ethnic map of great diversity. The style that emerged was one of extraordinary eclecticism which promoted receptivity to new ideas and innovative technology.

We will attempt to escape the strictures of single-purposed chronology: there is an end to the story, when the flood of the "Oriental" mode washes over greater China, but there are many beginnings.

THE CIVILIZATION OF SHANG

Any discussion of the Shang is a discussion focused on a symbolism which must remain unintelligible to us. There are certain structural themes, however, that we may derive, or at least impute, to this patterned symbolism. The ritual cycle created during the Shang period of dominance held within itself the celebration of the Shang lineage and heritage, and, in the calendrical system, the major steps towards civilization: literacy and predictive science.

The calendar, necessary for the proper arrangement of ceremonial obligations, was probably not significant to the ordering of agricultural activities. This was not irrigation agriculture, in which delicate control of artificial watercourses had to be seasonally adjusted. On the other hand, the calendar matured out of the folk wisdom of the farmer-peasant and was itself a product of careful observation and awareness of nature, of cycles of vegetational growth, of climate, and perhaps of the sky. The oracle bone inscriptions from which Tung-tso-pin and other specialists have reconstructed the calendrical computations made by the diviners and astronomers are filled with references to rain, clouds, mist, rainbows, snow, and dust-storms. The widespread observation of celestial phenomena and the means of calendrical notation is proven by the accurate reports of lunar eclipses which occurred in 1373, 1344, 1311, 1282, and 1279 B.C. Some of these eclipses would not have been visible from the site where the records were found.

There were two systems of computation which alternated during different "reign" periods, thus reinforcing the implication that the calendar was fundamental to the ceremonial cycle. The earlier system divided each day into seven periods from dawn to evening, but did not divide the night. Each day was named and fit into a "monthly" cycle of sixty-three days. In the so-called "progressive" calendar, the day was divided into ten hours, again only from morning until evening. The days were named within a ten day cycle, and these weeks were counted in a monthly cycle that alternated thirty-day periods with twenty-nine-day periods. Every once in a while, two thirty-day periods were run consecutively, so that at the end of twelve months there were 365.25 days in the year. This system was made more stable when the intercalary month was added at the end of certain years (roughly seven extra months within a nineteen-year cycle), so that no further adjustment was required.

The second major civilizing achievement—and in many ways the one which was for all time to separate man from the natural world, to give him the ability to modify it according to arbitrary conceptions of reality—was the achievement of literacy. Unfortunately we have as yet very imperfect knowledge of the origins and early development of the Chinese writing mode; when the script appears on the oracular bones used by the Shang diviners there are already about three thousand characters. Although the number of characters is overwhelming, there is internal evidence that the scribes did not have great familiarity with writing: there are many alternate forms of the same character and most of them are signs or emblems of proper names. Only about one-third of the characters have been deciphered, and these by a tortuous path of reconstruction based on the belief that the earliest Chinese writing was largely pictographic rather than phonological or ideographic.

The rigid formulae of divination do not permit flexibility in the sentences and reveal precious little in the sense of written "history." There is, however, a noticeable shift from private to public concerns, from questions about a given individual's well-being during the coming ten-day period, the weather for a planned hunting trip, or whether a painful toothache will be relieved, to queries about forthcoming harvests, eclipses, and predictions concerning the sex of children to be born into the ruling lineage.

Scapulimancy, or the technique of seeking oracular wisdom by "reading" the signs which appear on bones that are cracked and burned, is common to much of the world, and especially widespread in Asia. Although practised in the Neolithic villages of China, and not far removed from contemporary Chinese divination techniques, the use of oracle bones (properly speaking, tortoise shells) by the Shang had the added novelty of introducing written queries and answers. It may very well be that not only did the seeking of oracles help to incorporate the supernatural into the everyday, but that the writing itself was imbued with magical properties. It is very difficult to say who inscribed the shells. The characters were first painted on with a brush, but the carving which followed was probably done by a technician who was skilled in the use of bronze and jade knives. There is an individual style to the writing, sometimes it is delicate—almost in miniature—and at other times it is bold and sweeping. Frequently the name of the diviner is added to the inscription.

There is another feature of oracle script which impresses one with the awe of magical manipulation rather than the use of writing as a consciously devised, economical medium of communication. Almost all the divination texts which are written on turtle plastrons use the natural cracks of the shell as a mirror: i.e., the characters appear in standard form on one side of the center line but are reversed to face the line on the other side. This use of mirror-writing, so reminiscent of the divided *t'ao t'ieh* masks, could not have been derived from any literary expediency, but must have reflected a larger tradition of intellectual play with opposites that had a magical significance lost to us in the centuries of time.

While we were prevented from looking over the wall of

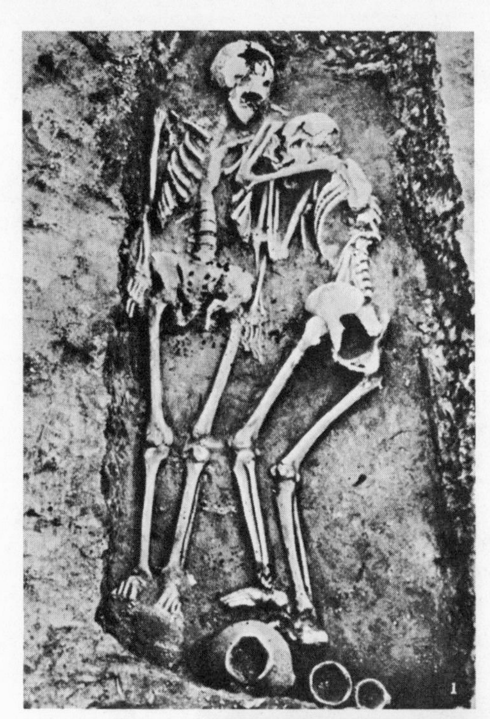

11. Multiple burials in the cemetery of Ch'i Chia, Kansu province.

12. Royal Shang tomb No. 1001 at Hou Chia Chuang, Honan province.

13. Shang bronze. Ceremonial covered vessel of the type *huo*, in the form of an elephant. Courtesy of the Smithsonian Institution, Freer Gallery of Art, Washington, D.C.

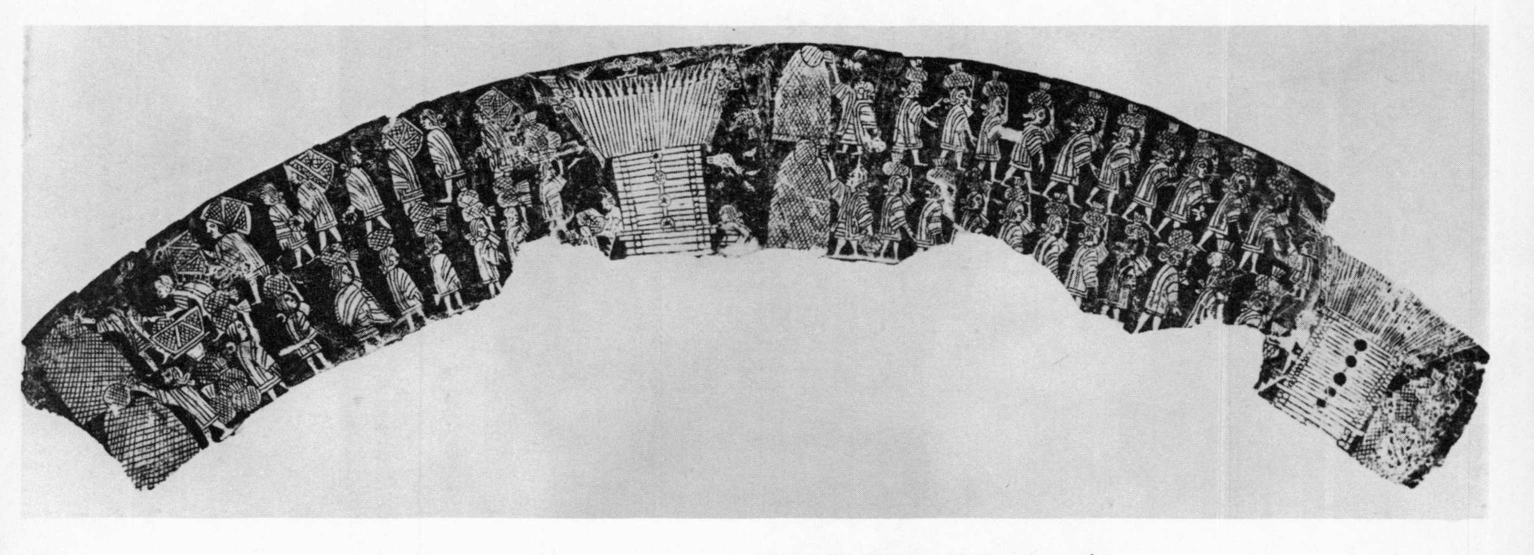

14. Detail of bronze drums from Shih Chai Shan, Yunnan province.

15. Bronze-casting molds from Hou Ma, Shansi. From Takeshi Sekino, *Arts of China, Neolithic Cultures to the T'ang Dynasty*, © 1968 by Kodansha International, Ltd.

16–17. Armrest, carved lacquer. Warring States period. Excavated from tomb No. 1, Ch'ang-t'ai-kuan, Hsin-Yang district, Honan. From Takeshi Sekino, *Arts of China, Neolithic Cultures to the T'ang Dynasty*, © 1968 by Kodansha International, Ltd.

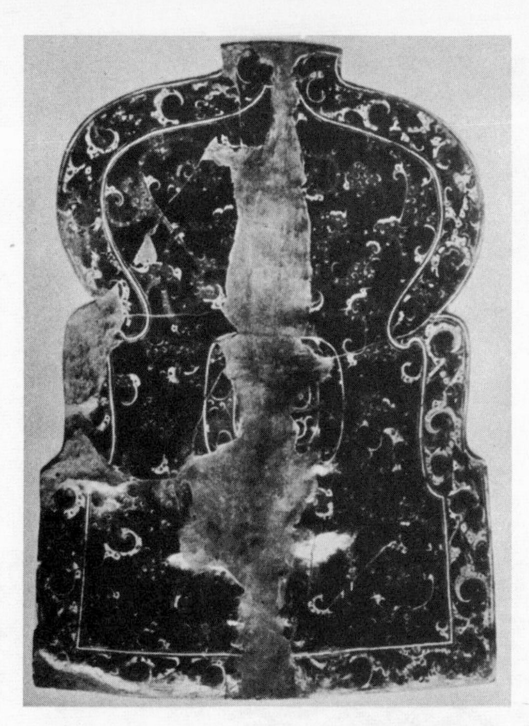

18. Inner surface of leather shield, red, yellow, and black lacquer. Warring States period. Excavated at Wu-li-p'ai, Ch'ang-sha municipality, Hunan. From Takeshi Sekino, *Arts of China, Neolithic Cultures to the T'ang Dynasty*, © 1968 by Kodansha International, Ltd.

19. Phoenixes, lacquered wood. Warring States period. Excavated at Ch'ang-t'ai-kuan, Hsin-Yang district, Honan. From Takeshi Sekino, *Arts of China, Neolithic Cultures to the T'ang Dynasty*, © 1968 by Kodansha International, Ltd.

20. Table, lacquered wood. Warring States period. Excavated at Ch'ang-sha municipality, Hunan. From Takeshi Sekino, *Arts of China, Neolithic Cultures to the T'ang Dynasty*, © 1968 by Kodansha International, Ltd.

21. Openwork panel, wood. Warring States period. Excavated at Yang-t'ien-hu Ch'ang-sha, Hunan. From Takeshi Sekino, *Arts of China, Neolithic Cultures to the T'ang Dynasty*, © 1968 by Kodansha International, Ltd.

22. Set of thirteen bells, bronze. (Reconstructed racks, lacquered wood.) Warring States period. Excavated from tomb No. 1, Ch'ang-t'ai-kuan, Hsin-Yang district, Honan. From Takeshi Sekino, *Arts of China, Neolithic Cultures to the T'ang Dynasty*, © 1968 by Kodansha International, Ltd.

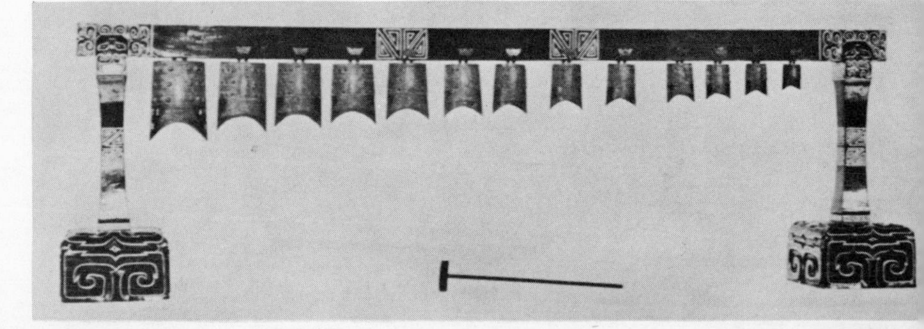

the city of Ao, we can move, with the last of the Shang chiefs, to the Great City of Yin at Anyang. The Chou Emperor Wu surveyed the bend in the Huan River that surrounds the village of Hsiao T'un and sang: "The heads of wheat are shaking, the grain and millet flowing . . . and in the distance is the mountain T'ai Hang." For 273 years this was the home of the living and the dead of the great family of Shang; today the sea of grain still bends in the wind; the three thousand years of history—of human toil—awesome as the fantastic world built here by the ancients.

Archeologists have now located the remains of villages and towns that spread over an area of twenty-four square kilometers. These clusters of workshops and the homes of artisans, farming hamlets, and cemeteries surrounded the city of Yin. The density of settlements becomes more scattered as we look away from the center, but in fact they were occupied prior to the move of the Shang ruling group to Hsiao T'un. These and similar villages specializing in bone-working and pottery-making were part of a network of circulating handicraft distribution during the time that Chengchou was a major center. These settlements came eventually to ring about the palaces of Yin, the royal tombs, and the thousands of sacrificial burials. The Shang ceremonial complex appears almost like an imposition, not as an energizing force, but perhaps foreshadowing the organizational rearrangements that were to come as the state itself developed.

Looking at Anyang as though from the air, there were two main centers of this complex: the Yin palaces, surrounded by habitation clusters, workshops and burials south of the Huan River; the royal cemetery at Hou Chia Chuang (Hsi Pei King) north of the river. Although the building of the living complex went on over hundreds of years, and there were many alterations and repairs, a general plan can be perceived: it is as though a straight line were drawn from north to south. To the north, the large buildings faced each other in regular rows on either side of this axis; amongst the buildings there were three large parallel gates. This entire section is separated from the southern section by a large platform (ten square meters) of pure yellow earth, and then once more the arrangement of structures is roughly oriented towards a north-south line. To the west is the area of the large temples, to the east the semi-subterranean dwellings and storage areas.

Let us start with the more familiar, the homes of the simple people—the servants and petty court officials, the people who guarded the storerooms, the tinkerers and folk who kept the palaces and temples in repair, the workers who provided the chiefly households with the material stuffs of everyday life. These people lived in rather large semi-subterranean houses. They were between four to five meters in diameter and were excavated about three meters below the ground surface, probably to provide protection from the bitter, dust-laden winds. The vertical walls had earthen stairways leading up to the exits, and most of them had stone-based center columns and frequently subsidiary posts that supported gabled thatch roofs. Many of the houses probably had wooden walls as well.

Smaller semi-subterranean units seem to have been tiny workshops. They are only two to four meters wide at the ground surface, and the inward sloping walls have footholds rather than stairways. Mats lined the earth floors, and the artifacts found in these pits—broken clay molds, pottery, arrowheads, shell vessels, smelting tools, deer antlers—seem to indicate that they were not used as dwelling-places.

There are even smaller pits which were used for storage. Some of these were granaries, but at least one was the repository of a library. Over seventeen thousand fragments of inscribed shell and two hundred complete tortoise plastrons were carefully put into this pit; incredibly, a man, perhaps the keeper, was buried here as well.

Running throughout the site at Hsiao T'un was an intricate tracery of ditches. Some of these were V-shaped, the sides constructed by the *hang-t'u* method of pounded earth, others show post impressions. Sandy deposits line the bottom of the channels, but we do not know the real function of the water system.

The above-ground buildings, usually called palaces, all followed generally similar principles of construction. Terrace-like foundations of *hang-t'u* were made smooth and hard. In at least one case, this was covered with a thin layer of lime plaster. Sometimes these raised foundations were more than a meter thick. Stone pillar-bases were placed on the foundation, although some were made of bronze. The pillars, frequently found as ash deposits, were made of wood. The largest building is sixty meters long, but others average twenty to thirty meters in length and are eight to nine meters wide. There is no question but that several of the buildings went through stages of reconstruction (perhaps after fires). Basement-like caves are frequently found under the foundations, and ash pits, that in one case contained layers of deer antler.

The continuity of lineage was expressed in the construction of these large buildings. Shih Chang-ju has suggested, on the basis of excavation and comparison with later textual material, that one building (24.4 × 8 m) with thirty-one pillars was divided into two sections: each section had its own central hall around which seven partitioned rooms were arranged. The entire structure probably supported a gabled thatch roof, and a series of steps led from the street to the central halls.

It is difficult to determine what segments of the lineages were housed in these dwellings. It is entirely possible that the two central "halls" were places of ancestor veneration. Over two hundred lineage names have been interpreted from the oracle inscriptions, but the use of multiple ceremonial titles and the instability of the early written characters may have inflated this number. It is more certain that the lineage had institutionalized to the point of tracing descent through five known generations, applying a collective term to each, and had established its origins from legendary ancestors who dissolved into the mythological past.

The integration of the sacred and profane which signalled the ascendancy of the ruling lineage to power was literally embodied in the house itself. When the ground was prepared for construction, a small pit was dug in the middle of the area, and a dog, or in some cases a small child, was buried. During the laying of the foundations, the three sacrificial animals of the Shang—the ox, the sheep, and the dog—were ritually killed and interred in the *hang-t'u*. When the pillar-bases were positioned, a human guardian, frequently in a kneeling attitude, was buried. When the doors were ready to be put into place, six pits were dug. Inside the door, five human beings, lying prone with their heads towards the center of the house, were buried in two of the pits. Outside the door, four guardians faced the street, ever alert to danger from without, with dagger-axes and shields.

As time went on, the inhabitants validated their status with further sacrificial ceremonies and surrounded the house with a great consecration of chariots and human beings. Seven of the important houses in the main compound of Hsiao T'un are surrounded by these sacrificial insignia: 852 human victims, 18 sheep, 35 dogs, 10 oxen, 15 horses, and 5 chariots.

Who were the nameless victims? Mostly they were young men, between twenty and thirty years old. It is possible to suggest that they were members of "outgroups," the social and ethnic groups upon whom the Shang chiefs depended, but whom they strove to define in non-kin terms of subordinate statuses. It has been the fashion to describe Shang society as a "slave" society, but there is absolutely no evidence of true, economically (i.e., agriculturally) productive slavery.

The only possible explanation within the traditional "slave" context comes if the underground structures previously described as tiny workshops were in fact slave quarters where a few foreigners with specialized talents lived who were put in domiciliary service to the ruling group. Possibly some of the people were taken from this group for sacrificial consecration of the buildings.

However, the growing elaboration of this relationship is better seen, not in the homes of the living, but of the dead.

In the Hou Chia Chuang cemetery there are well over one thousand graves in addition to the "Royal Tombs." The cemetery, like the residential area, is divided along a north-south axis, with four great tombs in the eastern sector and seven in the west. The larger, and perhaps earlier, of the tombs are cruciform in shape, while the others are rectangular. They all have stairs or sloping ramps which descend into the coffin chambers from the ground surface. The numerous small graves are arranged in rows running east–west, facing the great tombs. In some there are the headless skeletons of many hundreds of men, in others the heads are buried with the corpse after decapitation. Some are the final resting places of dismantled chariots, others of sacrificed animals.

We cannot describe the sounds—the screams and songs, the bells, dancing, and processionals, or the masses of people digging the great pits—some thirteen meters deep—or the smell of burning sacrifices or the colors of ceremonial costumes and blood. When the great tombs were built, the walls were straight, the bottoms flat. Stairways ran down the arms of the cross, but the southern entrance was smooth, as long as thirty meters. At the bottom of the pit, the main tomb chamber, also in the shape of a cross, was constructed in wood. The coffin was placed on a raised platform of white stone that was carved with tigers, owls, and oxen. Around the corpse, nine human guards and nine dogs were killed, in the center, in each corner, and in each of the cardinal directions. Rich bronzes and jades, musical instruments, pottery goblets, and ten human heads were placed in neat rows along the four tomb stairways. Along the southern ramp, a chariot and four horses, with fittings of bright bronze, and three men. Each man held a knife, a dagger-axe, and each had a bow and ten arrows.

There is an ambivalence—perhaps a purposeful expression of duality—in this kind of sacrifice. The victim must be honored, he cannot be despised. In the tomb he is fixed in an eternal relationship with the chief: he is a guardian, a warrior, a protector, a servant. His worth as a human being is celebrated by the sacrifice itself, but it is his status as an alien and a subordinate that endures.

The pattern of raiding and "warfare," of capturing men primarily for sacrifice (and probably horses as well), preceded the growth of a commercial network that fostered the tribute system of later years. Chou poetry and philosophy, with the institutionalized ideal of unity, glorified warfare, but for the Shang it was nothing more than another aspect of the search for legitimization of a stratified society. The machines of warfare were simple, and largely borrowed from the victims. Borrowed, unless we consider that before the Shang came to ascendancy they participated in the larger cultural configuration of Northern Asia and were allied to the nomads who were forever shifting across the ecological frontiers. For one thousand years they had been working out a cultural life-style of pastoralism which existed in symbiosis with the sedentary agriculturalists of the Huang plains.

The most deadly implement was the compound reflex bow, backed with horn and tipped with ivory, which required enormous strength and skill to achieve accuracy. It is difficult to imagine an untutored peasant wielding this bow, and thus it must have been the weapon only of the men from the ruling group who were trained in games and contests of hunting and archery during their adolescent years. Hand-to-hand combat was affected with the short dagger-axes of bronze and stone, and war-hatchets.

The Shang warriors—again we must think only of an elite —were protected with armor and shields of leather and helmets of bronze. The success of the Shang in capturing their victims must have rested on a short-lived supremacy of organization. This organization, soon to be far surpassed by the military system developed by the horse-riding nomads, was symbolically and realistically based on the war-chariot. The chariot was a slight wooden vehicle with two spoked wheels, drawn by a team of two horses. As we have seen, it was outfitted in splendor, and probably carried the battle-chief. The mobility afforded by the chariot aided the commander's ability to make decisions affecting the course of raids and brought inspiration to his followers.

One great burial at Hsiao T'un (and here it is impossible to guess who the victims were) seems to represent the fighting force commanded by the chief. The burial is composed of five units. In the center there are five horse chariots, a company of twenty-five men are near the chariots and 125 foot soldiers to the right of them. A single man, perhaps a chief, is buried alone to the right of the battalion; a group of sacrificed humans and animals are scattered behind the chariot burials.

More than anything else, the art style of the Shang created self-awareness and a lexicon that was capable of representing this identity across cultural barriers. It was a great art style. As we have seen, it pervaded all media and even today arouses in us an emotion of awe and a spirit of grandeur. In many aspects the great art style of the Shang is comparable to those of the formative periods of other civilizations—the Olmec and Chavin of the New World in particular, where they occur in sacred ceremonial settings. As expressions of ecumenical religions in Mexico and Peru, these styles wove the smaller parts of the social universe into a greater whole. The language of the Shang great art-style also moved outside its realm of origination, and channels of communication were opened between vastly different social spheres. These were to be exploited in the growing network of trade and were the cultural pathways that prepared China for the succeeding expansion of the Chou and for the rapid spread of iron metallurgy. After iron technology transformed some of the basic ecological relationships, political necessity required a transregional unification to supersede the mosaic, and semi-isolated, village way of life.

SOUTHWEST CHINA

Throughout mainland Southeast Asia there are several important Bronze Age cultures that share a great ecumenical tradition; in China itself, localized expressions of this tradition flourished in Szechwan and in Yunnan. We are able to give archeological identity to three of the historically best known cultures, Shu, Pa and Tien. The heterogeneous environmental setting of these cultures was at once the cause of differentiation, but also facilitated the spread of the greater tradition. The alternations of extraordinary mountains, high grassland valleys and passes, and low-lying alluvial plains along the many mountain-fed streams were fundamental to indigenous adaptations.

We have seen the earlier exploitation of the vast region by a tenacious forest efficiency, but within this pattern there were refractions that represent the micro-specializations, if not of basic technological relationships then of the intensity with which they were applied to the environment. One of these differences was between the mixed economy of the western mountain zone and the sedentary (or partially sedentary) way of life that was supported by fishing and collecting in river valleys and on hill slopes. In eastern Szechwan by 1000 B.C. a rudimentary social stratification appeared, but the only indicator of the stratification is the accumulated "wealth" represented by luxury art products, fine pottery, jades, and a few bronze arrow points found in burials.

SHU

By contrast, the Chengtu plain was peopled by tribes that were knit together in a loose confederacy dominated by the Shu. Whether the Shu initially represented a lineage, clan, or even several social groups, we cannot say. However, it is clear that the indigenous nature of gradual stratification of ethnic or social units was stimulated by a far-flung commerce and exploitation of natural resources such as tin and salt; it is also possible that men of Shu, not permanently tied to the land by agricultural obligations, served as "mercenaries" for the western Chou. Many of the bronze objects were imports from Chou workshops and must have had value which can only be expressed as monetary.

Of the many surface finds, burials, and habitation sites recorded for the Chengtu region, perhaps the most revealing is that of T'ai-p'ing-Ch'ang, first investigated in 1933. The site is on a hilltop, forty or fifty feet above the surrounding Hanchou plain. Although the plain is filling in with the silt brought down from the mountain irrigation system, the hills are being eroded, and so the relics of life of three thousand years ago are exposed to twentieth-century eyes. The initial discovery of finely cut stone discs, squares, and knives was made at the bottom of an irrigation ditch that was first used during the Ming dynasty. An ancient pit had been uncovered by the ditch; it was about 2.3 m × 1 m in area and 1 m deep. After the pit was dug, its sides were lined with vertical rows of stone discs and twenty stone discs were placed flat on top. The contents of the pit were extraordinary: nearly one hundred fragments of stone rings, mostly of jade, over eighty geometrically shaped flakes of jade, jade and turquoise beads, and knives fashioned of many different kinds of beautiful stone. This treasury was in the midst of the mundane debris of several contemporaneous hamlets on the raised terraces between the Yatze and Mamu rivers. The pottery found in the hamlets was in the village tradition and not elaborate: the vessel shapes simple and completely utilitarian and the firing techniques not carefully controlled.

Nearby, north of the present city of Chengtu, a unique burial complex at Yang-tze-shan was probably of the same period as the Hanchou occupation. Here, a tamped earthen structure was constructed to incorporate many burials. This great platform is ten meters high and covers an area over 140 meters. Jades again appear in abundance, but are strangely associated with undistinguished pottery even in this highly ceremonial context.

Is it possible to find historically valid meaning in the extensive use of jade in the death ritual? Here of course we are balancing on the tightrope of uncertain ethnohistory, since we are in an arena of great cultural blending. However, these archeological "cultures" of 1000–500 B.C. were in the process of being woven into a stylistic fabric. The process was arrested by the impact of Ch'in transgressions which forced the different ethnic groups to rigidify and revitalize their own sources of integrity.

It may be that the ideology of the past has been brought forward in the folklore of the present. The symbolic content of jade is manifold in Southwest China, frequently bearing the duality of mountains and water, and consequently of male and female. The rich, well-watered plain of Chengtu offered opportunities for agricultural experimentation and exploitation. This experimentation is embodied in the legend of the engineer Li Ping, who helped Emperor Yü conquer the mighty streams that descend from the Tibetan massif. In the absence of the physical data of archeology we may perhaps interpolate the ritual use of jade in a double context

—that of an idealized mountain worship, common throughout Southeast Asia, and of the beginnings of irrigation agriculture which necessitated both manipulation of the rivers and "control" of the rains.

There are only a few discoveries that help us discern the image of the Shu. Again, the Han quasi-history is helpful, for it is recorded that the earliest "king" of Shu was Ts'an Ts'ung, but that a later chief, Tu Tzu, abdicated to Pieh Ling. Pieh Ling was a man of the Ch'u, and adopted the name of Kai Ming. He established a dynasty that continued until its defeat by the Ch'in in 316 B.C. The legend of Pieh Ling may in fact represent the expansion of the agricultural innovation from east to west, stimulating the adoption of cultivation by indigenous tribes wherever the new technique was feasible and advantageous. It is doubtful that a movement of people was involved. However, the nature of the economy is still unclear; continued contact with the steppe peoples suggests that the Shu may at first have been an animal-dependent group that came to mediate between the agriculturalists and pastoralists.

One of the most important discoveries in the Chengtu region was a "hoard" of twenty-one bronze pieces found in the Penghsien district. A great pottery urn was uncovered by railroad workers in 1961, near the Chingpai River. Inside the urn there were eight vessels, several daggers and axes, a socketed adze, and a long leaf-shaped spearhead. One of the bronze vessels was a great *lei* of sixty-eight centimeters in height. Two smaller *lei* had covers which had been cast with the most incredible figures: each has a horned monster figure squatting with its feet outstretched, and the long serpentine tail of the monster curls around the rim. One figure has a short row of flanges projecting along the ridge of its back, each covered, like the tail, with a cowrie-like motif. Dragon-shaped handles decorated with linear *t'ao t'ieh* masks divide the body of one vessel, marking the "mirror" against which a pair of dragons confront each other. The other small *lei* has a pair of elephants placed over the paired dragons, and the inner spaces are filled with graceful, crested birds. The weapons are decorated, sometimes with typical eastern *t'ao t'ieh*, sometimes with lizards; but two are inscribed in an archaic script. Elsewhere in the Chengtu region, scattered but undocumented finds of bronzes add to this sense of the eclectic: a *ting* with a bird's-head cover, a loop-handled knife, bronze seals engraved with the enigmatic pictographs and a group of spearheads, some socketed and some with perforations but all characterized by the decorative motif of the tiger.

Farther west, near Kan Tzu, a series of burials contained bone tools, pottery, and bronze swords, bracelets, bells, and belt hooks. The bronzes were all in the mode of the art of the steppes, but with distinctive characteristics that point to Yunnan and the contemporary Pa culture of Chungking.

Perhaps the clue to the rise of the Shu lies in their script, and in the apparent selectivity with which they accepted imported products and symbols, incorporating them into their own ideological style. The development of written notation may have been a concomitant of the commercial nature of Shu contact with other tribes and ethnic groups. Located at prime salt and tin deposits, Shu chieftains were in a position of exploiting these resources and possibly the people who worked them. This then was not a land-based feudal relationship, but was one that placed the Shu in an extraordinary role as middlemen. We do not know the extent of trade, but silks found in the Deccan and in Central Asia may have come from Szechwan; spices from Szechwan were famous in Cantonese cuisine; elephants, varnish, hemp, and possibly glass were among the goods carried over the major waterways from India, and across the "Burma Road," the trans-Himalaya passes.

PA

The vivid eclecticism, the multi-ethnicity of Szechwan becomes more exciting as we look to the narrow Chialing River valley that runs north-south through the center of the province. Here dwelt the people that the Han Chinese called "Pa." Two cemeteries have been discovered, and the style of burial, in addition to the artifacts found in the graves, delineates a unique configuration of cultural behavior. These cemeteries, one in the north and the other near Chungking, both contain burials in narrow cedarwood canoes. These are interred in shallow pits arranged in rows along the river bank. The ritual focus on the river which bears the individual from a familiar life through the unexperienced courses of death is emphasized by the careful placement of valuable grave-goods within the boat-coffin. Bronze weapons were put at the head of the corpse, and pottery and bronze vessels were arranged at the feet. Axes, spearheads, and seals were engraved with a combination of archaic Chinese characters and as yet undeciphered glyphs. Willow-leaf-shaped swords frequently carried the insignia of the tiger, the animal's head or the whole body, often patterned with intricate designs. Other bronze objects included belt hooks, mirrors, and arrowheads. Some iron axes were also buried. Preservation was excellent and remains of silk and hempen fabrics, bamboo and lacquered utensils, and beads of ceramic and glass were still in the coffins. A system of sequence dating was attempted, showing that the burials spanned the period between ca. 500 B.C. and the Ch'in incursions of 200 B.C.

Once again we find the marvelous selectivity guided by fashion and taste, the intrinsic value of objects as items of prestige but perhaps also of ceremonial significance. The shape of weapons borrowed from the Chungyuan and from the Hanshui Valley, the ornaments from the steppes, but, even when borrowed, imprinted with the mark of the Pa and the script they shared with the Shu. The unity of these two social groups is to be seen in the pervasive emblem of the tiger. Historical writings of the Han tell the story of the White Tiger and attribute this myth to the Pa. The origin myth describes the unification of the Pa clans under the leadership of the fictive Lin Chun, who was transformed into a great white tiger. The celebration of origin took the form of human sacrifice. The White Tiger drinks of the blood of the Pa and is sustained.

Although at first an import, the production of bronze soon became a local craft. Not only is the alloy quite different from that of the north, containing higher percentages of tin, but the shape of many implements is unique to the southwest, and the design motifs and script are indigenous. The very early appearance of cast iron knives and other weapons proves localized familiarity with the techniques of metallurgy.

For the Pa, as with the Shu, the absence of the ruins and debris of large settlements argues against developed, intensive agriculture. The traditional and legendary representation of Pa fighting men, their "wild songs and dances," can be seen portrayed on the bronze drums of Tien. As we explore the life of Tien, in Yunnan, we must bear in mind that the Pa and the Shu were brought into the sphere of the Southeast Asian Bronze Age, sometimes called "Dongson," and may well have performed a critical role as cultural "brokers" with the northern centers of emerging civilization.

TIEN

Sixteen people, some on horseback, some on foot, are leaving the village and moving towards the fields. In front a mounted rider, followed by a man carrying a large plowshare; behind him are four men bearing a sedan chair in which rides a woman wearing golden clothing, her hair hangs long. She looks down at a person kneeling in front of her. To her left are three people. One carries a sack of grain slung across his shoulders, a woman looks up at the notable in the sedan chair and raises her hands in greeting, a third squats on the ground spreading out baskets of food and holding a basin. Others in the procession hold long wooden tools in their hands, and at the end of the line a woman balances a basket on her head.

A large granary constructed of interlocking logs stands at the edge of a village. The wooden plank floor is raised above the ground to avoid the damp, and a short flight of steps leads into the granary. To the left are three reed huts where bags of woven grass filled with grain were placed during the harvesting. Now one woman removes these storage bags and puts them on the ground. Nine others have already taken filled bags out of the beehive-shaped shelters. The women all wear their hair piled high in a bun on top of the head. They walk to the granary, carrying baskets on their heads. At the entrance a man stands ready to load the baskets into the storeroom. Another group of women moves towards the temporary granaries, holding empty baskets and the plaited-reed rings that will support them when they are heavy with grain.

In the plaza there is a wooden platform raised off the ground on large tree posts. The platform, which is the height of a man, is surrounded by a railing and has a stairway leading up to it. There is a wooden house built at the back of the platform; from each protruding end of the ridgepole is hung the head of an ox. On the platform many men and women, dressed in trailing garments, have gathered to dance while a group of musicians prepares to play their reed instruments, chiming stones, and kettledrums. Near the stairway people are busy cooking; benches and eating utensils have been set out on the platform. Cows, pigs, and goats are tethered underneath. In the single window of the house a human head is suspended, severed from the sacrificed body.

Thus the people of Tien, the first spring sowing of the

fields, the harvest, the sacrificial feasting; seen not through alien eyes, but with the truer vision of the participant. These are vignettes of the ritual calendar, cast in bronze and thus come down through the centuries. The Han historian, Ssu Ma Chien, heard of the people of the southwest, perhaps from travellers and traders:

> There are dozens of chiefs ruling among the southwest barbarians, but the most important is the ruler of Yeh-lang. To the west of Yeh-lang live the chiefs of the Mi-mo, of which the most important is the ruler of Tien. North of Tien live numerous other chiefs, the most important being the ruler of Ch'iung-tu. All of the tribes ruled by these chiefs wear their hair in the mallet-shaped fashion, work the fields and live in settlements. Beyond them to the west, in the region from Tung-shih east to Yeh-yü, are the tribes called Sui and K'un-ming, whose people all braid their hair and move from place to place with their herds of domestic animals, having no fixed homes and no chieftains. Their lands measure several thousand *li* sq. Northeast of the Sui live twenty or thirty chiefs, the most important being those of Hsi and To-tu. Among the numerous chiefs northeast of Tso those of Jan and Mang are most important. Some of their people live a settled life on the land, while others move from place to place. Their territory is west of the province of Shu. Northeast of Jan and Mang are numerous other chiefs, the most important being the ruler of Po-ma. All of them belong to the Ti tribe. These are all the barbarian groups living in the area southwest of Pa and Shu.
>
> *Shih Chi*
>
> (after the translation by Watson, 1958)

Ssu Ma Ch'ien was correct: the many ethnic groups of Yunnan took on their separate identities as they developed in counterpoint to each other and to the centers of civilization in Southeast Asia, Ch'u, and eventually Northern China. Before the appearance of Tien and the other stratified societies of Yunnan, the region was covered with the vast mantle of the forest efficiency, differentiated as the topography alternated between deep river valleys and high mountain ranges. This was a pattern that followed ecological zones rather than arbitrary boundaries, and the unity was with Southeast Asia.

There were three major foci of technological experimentation once the forest efficiency had allowed the people to gain a secure foothold in Yunnan. Although these are local adaptations, each with its own history, it may be helpful to view them chronologically, as though on a continuum.

Around the great lake of Tien, near the city of Kunming, two specialized adaptations took place, both of which supported permanent settlements. On the lake shores intensive mollusk collecting was supplemented by casual cultivation, and on the slopes of the hills surrounding the lake the people farmed more intensively. The major crop was wheat. The villages were not large, and the crafts were distinctly local; the pottery was tempered with crumbled bits of shell and sand, and frequently a shell was used to draw simple geometric designs in the wet clay. The houses were permanent, with tiled roofs. The tools were made of stone and probably of wood.

In the northwest of Yunnan there was a settlement of agriculturalists as yet seen imperfectly by archeological remnants alone. The ancient village of Hai Men K'ou, in the district of Chien Ch'uan, was comprised of houses constructed on piles. This was probably done to keep the waters from flooding and to control the mosquitoes, but also perhaps provided a shelter for the family pigs. Living right on the mud flats of the river, fishing and mollusk gathering were important activities for the children and adults, but the major resource of the villagers lay in the surrounding fields. The land was multi-cropped; wheat, millet, and rice were all cultivated by the farmers. The implements of agricultural production were of stone, but some natural copper was hammered into cutting implements, fishhooks, and ornaments.

The third focus of archeologically recognizable intensive settlement is in the Tali district around Lake Ehr. Here the experiment with agricultural technology was carried forward as a new ecology was created. The early hamlets were small and dispersed over the hill slopes. The houses were at first semi-subterranean, but later were built above ground. The locally produced pottery was of the typical southwestern redware and decorated with simple incisions. The slopes were hacked into terraces with short stone hoes and paved with small stones for the foundations of the houses. Agriculture was extensive; wheat and probably yams were the staple crops. Gradually, however, the stone tools were replaced with iron; sickles and plowshares of metal increased the potential for working the soil; then the farmers began to extend their terraces, build balks of earth between them, and dig ditches through which they could guide the water running down the hills after each rain. Only then did the ecology of the region begin to change, only then did cultivation incorporate more and more land while it supported greater populations. Not only were the people absorbed into the agricultural way of life, but the native metallurgical industry marked the beginning of occupational specialization and the success of irrigation destroyed the egalitarianism of the Neolithic, providing a focus for wealth in terms of the accumulation of land and water rights.

We are now prepared for the Tien but must remain in suspenseful disappointment. Only burial grounds have been discovered, and we wonder where are the cities, the market places, the castles and fortresses, where the literature and the drama? Ssu Ma Ch'ien (or his reporter) gave us several clues; perhaps the most obvious was the inability of this most perspicacious historian to adequately grasp anything that was outside his experience as a man of Han. To write about the societies of the southwest in political terms was probably correct, for this would have been recognizable to the Han, whereas the content of culture would have escaped them.

In fact there were no cities with dense populations; these were truly the barbarians—not in the pejorative sense of later Chinese terminology, but similar to the barbarian populations of pre-Classical Europe. The stratification that seems to make itself so obvious in the cemeteries was horizontal, perhaps caste-like or perhaps based on kin affiliation and the status of different kin groups. One analyst, M. von Dewall, has suggested that there were three main groups, the clan chieftains, the warrior nobility, and the warrior farmers who lived in the smaller villages surrounding the "royal" cemetery of Shih Chai Shan. Certainly the first two groups can be validated.

A chief was buried in a lacquered coffin with the jewelry and utensils of gold that were restricted to his use; even his iron and bronze swords were sheathed in gold foil. Interred only with the chiefs were the full regalia of horsemanship: the bridles, buckles, bells, and crossbows. Strangely, the chief's tomb also carried into eternity the reminders of the soil, plowshares, hoes, sickles, and the axes, adzes, and chisels of the everyday workman. And the profits of his mercantilism were there also, the bronze containers with hundreds of the precious cowrie-shell money, and exotic imports from Indo-China, Central Asia, and Northern China. In this way the tomb of the chief was imbued with the life of all the society. By contrast, the very specialized group of warrior nobility was accompanied in death by their weapons, mostly of iron, sometimes combined with decorative bronze hilts, armor, pretty ornaments for their belts, and the fine bronzes, lacquer ware, and pottery that constituted their reward for service or their wealth.

One must ask, were these really "warriors"? Perhaps they were in the sense that they secured the trade routes exploited by the chiefs. And, just as in barbarian Europe, the greater part of the population remains barely identified, toiling in the fields, but joyously celebrating with their chiefs the rituals that reinforced the stratified nature of their society: here a common belief system, a shared world-view, as shown so vividly in the bronzes. There was more unity in this ideology than in the technologically differentiated urban centers. Even the metallurgist was fully aware of the entire range of cultural behavior, for there was nothing sacred to his patron that was not sacred also to him.

We will have to leave the southwestern cultures with a very uneasy feeling. Our perception of the style of life is vague and shadowy. The only confidence we have is of an extraordinary heterogeneity that encouraged the easy flow of materials and ideas. These were the times of epics, but it remains for the ethnohistorian to discover who were the heroes. Although undoubtedly responsible for transmitting much of the material content of northern civilization, they remained uncomprehended and thus never truly confronted.

WESTERN CHOU

In the Weishui Valley of Shensi the people who had come to be called "Western Chou" had their homeland. We have looked at the villages where people farmed and kept mixed herds of animals, and we have seen the small towns such as K'e Hsing Chuang. We wondered at the absence of the sparks that would signify to us the incipient vitality of the Western Chou civilization.

Our vision was myopic. We failed to see the cultural implications of the exploitation of a variegated environment by a diversified technology. We did not recognize the wandering shepherds who were only in part tied to the villages but who for much of their lives moved among the valley grasslands of the southern mountains, reaching towards Szechwan and Tibet, but outward also along the Kansu corridor to the west, where they came to intermingle with the populations that were beginning to use the mobility of mounted horses to extend the pastoral way of life.

We previously mentioned the Karasuk cultures of the Minusinsk basin, agriculturalists and sheepherders who had already incorporated a simple metal industry into their craft repertoire. The small angulated knives, sometimes with animal-head handles, seem to be derived from the copper daggers of the Angara-Baikal region, and are found scattered throughout Mongolia and Northern China. The Tagar culture that replaced the Karasuk about 800 B.C. represented a total reworking of the ecology as the horse-riding nomads began to spread across the steppelands, frequently setting up and supporting small enclaves of metalworkers who produced bronze objects in which the animals of the forest—the bear, boar, and ibex—shared favor as art motifs with the curled animals and birds' heads that played so important a part in the art of the Scyths of south Russia. The hoards of bronzes that are discovered by the archeologist may have been the stock kept by the bronze-caster-merchants who sold them to a wide market. Some of them undoubtedly were brought into the Shensi heartland.

As the Sacae drew in from Central Asia, and the steppe peoples of the southeast settled in the Yenesei River region, the people of the northern Altai with their own metal industry were slowly brought into relationship with the nomads, the mounted pastoralists of the high mountains. In the Maeimir phase of Altai occupation during the seventh and sixth centuries B.C., the horse and harness burials and the bell-shaped bronze helmets are strongly reminiscent of the grand tombs of Northern China.

The peoples of Shensi, at 1000 B.C., were heir to generations of familiarity and interaction with the steppe cultures, but because of their uniquely diversified ecological situation, they shared as well in the great streams of civilization that were beginning to surface in northern Southeast Asia. In northeast Thailand and near Saigon, Vietnam, at about 2500 B.C., local bronze-casters were making socketed tools with two-piece molds, and by the first millennium B.C., Yunnan and Szechwan were brought into the Southeast Asian sphere through a far-flung trade in the raw materials and refined products of this metallurgical industry. And in the east were the Shang, explosively original but doomed to fail in the leap to statehood.

Thus were the pre-dynastic Chou (the Chi lineage) surrounded by the excitement of innovative technology and revolutionary socio-ecological changes.

The first glimpses of the transformation stimulated amongst the Chou are at the ancient settlements in the vicinity of the modern village of Chang Chia P'o near Sian. One of the earliest of these seems already to have taken on the characteristic diversification of occupations. There are bone workshops where arrowheads and hairpins were manufactured, and foundries in which the fittings for chariots were made in piece molds. Other bronze objects were produced in the factories, including knives with concave blades and square-looped handles. The settlement of Chang Chia P'o was one of a cluster that surrounded the early centers of Feng and Hao—known in the historical records as the "capitals" of the Western Chou. At other small towns there are workshops that made pottery and some kilns that manufactured tiles for roofing, dwellings, and temples. The tiles are fired at high temperatures and made of fine clay; the builders laid the flat tiles on wet clay plaster and joined them with small, semi-cylindrical tiles. The smoky-blue roofs must have softened the appearance of the bleak mud houses and dusty streets of the village.

The pottery found at Chang Chia P'o is interesting when examined in chronological sequence. At first it is a village craft, producing serviceable but undistinguished greyware that cannot be easily differentiated from the ceramics of hundreds of years of Neolithic tradition. After intensive contact with the east, especially with the superb Shang potters, improvements were made in the kilns, and molded vessels take their place with the more common beaten ware. Eventually, when trade relations were opened up with the southeast, the famed glazed stoneware of Kiangsu was imported into Chou homes in Shensi.

Although there has not been extensive excavation in the Feng River region, at least one significant innovation in agricultural technology has been discovered. The farmers of the loessland began to dig wells, lining the shafts with great ceramic rings to prevent the walls from collapsing. We do not know the mechanism by which water was raised from these wells, but it is the first attempt to manipulate sources outside of the uncertain rainfall.

Through the screen of written Chou history, five or six administrative centers appear in shadowy outline. They were all in the Weishui Valley of Shensi, but only the last two have found archeological credibility. The capitals of Feng and Hao were situated on the west and east banks of the river and were occupied for approximately 350 years. It was from Hao that Wu Wang, headman of the Chi, led the first successful expeditions against the Shang, and in 1122 B.C. "captured" their prince, Wu Keng. In Hao, a man named Chen cast a bronze cauldron to be used during the feasting that celebrated the event. Wu Weng prepared a grand sacrifice to his father, and the *kuei* was inscribed with a long, seventy-eight-character hymn validating the lineage and its ascent to political dominance. Chen cast the cauldron in the style that he understood, with animal-headed birds and a shape that had never been seen in the east but was not foreign to the steppelands.

This preliminary attempt at expansion and assimilation through conquest was not a simple victory. The peoples of

Honan, Shantung and Anhwei, who were only lightly enmeshed in the Shang complex, rejected and rebelled against the Chou. It was not until many years later that Chou Kung was able to overcome this resistance by formulating and reformulating ties between the socio-cultural groups of Northern China, eventually reaching into Mongolia and southwards towards the Yangtze.

As these ties began to have political reality, Chou Kung moved his administration to Loyang, in western Honan, where he built a city at a site of a Shang settlement. But the many other centers of emerging civilization continued to function as discrete focal points of economic and political activity and retained their essential integrity.

The intensification of external relations that perhaps stimulated the internal social and political changes of Western Chou can be seen only partially, since there has not as yet been a major excavation of Western Chou settlements and we must rely on the cemetery remains. The tombs in the Feng area are arranged in groups, although there is no standard method of interment. The dead were placed in wooden coffins and shallow pits. Those who carried the prestige of lineage—and, perhaps at the beginning, those who had acquired special recognition as leaders in raiding and warfare—were buried in large tomb chambers, always accompanied by a dog and a great number of bronze weapons. This emphasis on warfare in early Chou life is reflected by many experiments with armaments, the new forms of daggers that were perforated for more secure hafting and the attempt to increase the efficiency of the weapons by attaching two or more cutting implements to the same shaft. The short dagger was lengthened into a sword, and towards the end of this period, iron was cast into blades that were attached to bronze handles. Without doubt, the steady pressure from rapidly expanding nomadic pastoralists of the steppes forced the Chou to adopt stratagems for military mobilization that were politically administered. Some of the inscriptions, if taken literally, imply that the success of the Chou was not in battle —which never lasted longer than one day—but in their ability to confront the enemy with thousands of men.

The funerary rites included mortuary feasting, and pairs of bronze vessels were put into each tomb; sometimes two cooking vessels, two containers (one still had the remains of an entire pig's head inside), two wine-warming vessels or a pair of goblets. There were probably great parades—perhaps resembling the grand tour made by the entourage bearing the dead chiefs of the pastoralists—led by fantastically caparisoned horses and chariots. The most beautiful of the breed wore headpieces of bronze, decorated with animal-masks, long bronze nosepieces, intricate leather harnesses with bronze fastenings, bells and tassels, and muzzles made of strings of the precious cowrie shell. Even the tails of the animals were braided with cowrie strings and plaques of carved shell. The horses were sacrificed in only seven of the several hundred graves, along with the chariots they drew. The chariot itself was somewhat different from the Shang chariot, with special axle-caps of bronze and a wheel with twenty-one spokes and conical-shaped hubs. It may have been a more versatile vehicle, able to traverse difficult terrain.

The dead were dressed richly and laid out with jade objects that were carefully prescribed. Rectangular plaques were placed by the head, rings of jade in the ears and mouth, belt pendants in the shape of fish, dragons, cicadas and silkworms, all decorated with finely incised linear designs. Strings of shell, bone, pottery, bronze, and glass beads were hung around the neck, placed on the stomach and near the head of the person. These strings are often divided into segments by markers of jade and shell, or several strings are attached to each other by short branches that occur at regular intervals. These beads, like the cowrie shells, may have been a form of currency, part of the worldly treasure buried with the wealthy. The scarcity of the commodity argues for its use as money. If this is the case, then the entire ritual is one which is devised to reinforce the social and economic stratification achieved by the individual during his lifetime. Because of the absence of human sacrifice, and the long inscriptions on bronze vessels which tell of appointments to political office, of economic rewards for service, of military victories, we know that these burial rites are no longer concerned with the paraphernalia of religion or the validation of ancestry. One would have to look elsewhere for the symbols of religiosity, the fossilized evidence of competing value and cosmological systems. Unfortunately we are troubled in this search both by the lack of archeological exploration and the codification of these systems in the early texts of Confucius and the burgeoning schools of philosophy. It is thus impossible to test the codes against reality.

In the *Shih Chi* we read that the legendary Emperor Yü spent thirteen years travelling through the nine provinces. On land he travelled by cart, over water he went by boat, he wore cleated shoes to climb the mountains and used sled to move over the swamps. Everywhere he went he built roads and opened canals. He constructed canals leading off the Huangho and joined them with the Chi, Huai, and Ssu rivers. These canals passed through the "states" of Sung, Cheng, Ch'en, Ts'ai, Ts'ao, and Wei. In the land of Ch'u he built two canals, one went from the Han River to the ancient lake of Yunmeng, and in the east he connected the Huai River with the Yangtze. In Shu, the engineer Li Ping opened up channels for the two rivers from the mountains to cut across the Chengtu plain.

We need not give the legend a literal interpretation, for it expresses a more significant reality: the multiplicity of cultures, the pulse of the life, and excitement of the times.

"I made a coat of lotus and water-chestnut leaves,
and gathered lotus petals to make myself a skirt.
I will no longer care that no one understands me,
as long as I can keep the sweet fragrance of my mind."

Chü Yüan, third century B.C.

CHAPTER VI

North and South

We can return to the geography of the *Yü Kung* for the lesson it contains. Earlier, we examined the description of the many provinces—soils, water, crops, and people. In introducing each there is a statement which gives the physical boundaries of the province: the south of Mount Hua and the Blackwater River were the boundaries of Liangchou; the Ching Mountains and the southern slopes of Mount Huang were the boundaries of Chingchou; the Huang River and the sea were the boundaries of Yangshou, etc. These are true boundaries, the political delimitation of territories; geography was no longer a matter of environment and the natural order but of conflict and warfare. This is the time also when the people began to impose their will on the waterways, which had been used primarily for transportation. Although the major change was in the quantity and kind of cargo carried by the rafts and barges (basic foodstuffs increasingly moved along with raw materials and manufactured products), small canals were constructed to divert water into the cultivated fields.

Agricultural activity increased, but the yield was still unpredictable and at little more than the Neolithic level of per capita production. It was said that in good years the yield could be four times the average, that in poor years it might drop to one-fifth the average. While the techniques of agriculture did not change, the fundamental technology did change when the introduction of iron tools made it possible for more and more land to be brought under cultivation. In the historical writings, the theme of establishing boundaries is inextricably bound with that of land reclamation. This meant incorporating, sometimes by use of armed force, the "no-man's lands," the wastelands, into the agricultural ecology. This process was occurring in the north, where the small states that had formed out of aggregates of agricultural communities consciously broadened the belt of cultivated land that separated them from the pastoralists, developing the barbarian markets into centers of communication by settling soldiers on the frontiers.

To the south, the expanding incorporation of land was epitomized by the territorial spread of the Ch'u civilization throughout Central China. Here the configuration of intensive labor applied to irrigated fields, the widespread use of iron tools, and the emergence of a literati so totally alienated from the technology of subsistence as to "no longer care that no one understands me."

We have seen the florescence of civilizational styles in the west and in the southwest regions of China. In the north during the fifth century B.C., the scene becomes more exciting but less filled with cultural contrasts. Ch'in, Wei, Chao, Yen, Ch'i, Han, Sung, Lu, and many other aggregates of population took on political definition as they competed with each other and with the pastoralists for land to put into cultivation. The "city-state" pattern was elaborated, town walls and fortifications constructed, palatial buildings, factories, and roads built.

Before looking through the very incomplete album of

"snapshots" that must stand for civilizations, it will be useful to briefly mention the known history of iron technology in China. Iron facilitated an already emergent way of life; it did not create a revolution, nor did it usher in a new "age." The manufacture of iron made the already existing specialization of industrial occupations even more pronounced, while iron tools of production became part of a new set of ecological and socio-political relationships.

J. Needham has traced many literary references to iron ore, mining and smelting, and the use of iron weapons and implements. Amongst the earliest are texts which attribute the casting of iron cauldrons to the fifth century B.C., and others which tell of iron weapons. Texts of the fourth and third centuries B.C. mention the abundance of iron in the lands of the Shu and the Pa; Mencius relates a story about Hsü Hsing, saying that he "cooks his food in pans of metal and pottery and ploughs with an iron ploughshare." And in the *Kuan Tzu* of the third century, B.C. there is a passage referring to the regulation of taxes on iron: ". . . every woman needs a needle and a knife, every farmer a hoe and a ploughshare, and every cartwright his axe, saw, and chisel."

Although the Hittites had been fashioning brittle weapons of wrought iron as early as 1250 B.C., the iron implements of fifth-century-B.C.-China—now archeologically substantiated—were cast into the shapes of axes, adzes, chisels, spades, sickles, and hoes. Wooden plow-blades were tipped with iron. Once again, the pattern of interlocking techniques can be seen as the knowledge and methods involved in finding and mining ores and the highly refractory clays needed for crucibles; having the means to construct and control furnaces capable of attaining high temperatures, the early use of coal as a fuel and the use of water-power to strengthen the blast created by the bellows were combined into a single technology.

THE NORTHERN STATES

In the region of Hsin T'ien, in the southern part of contemporary Shansi, two ancient cities have been excavated near Hou Ma Chen. Both were walled, and there is a trace of an inner wall enclosing platforms on which stood extensive tiled buildings of wood. These secluded buildings were reached by ramps running up from the streets in which the ruts worn by the passing two-wheeled carriages can still be seen. The entire area may have been surrounded by a moat, separating these rich dwelling quarters and storehouses from the working population who clustered about the central place and lived in and amongst the workshops. One of the most interesting features of the Hsien T'ien villages are those specialized in metalworking, where individual shops apparently produced a limited range of objects; some manufacturing chariot fittings, others making coinage, and others tools or vessels. There are villages that specialized in ceramic production and many bone workshops. All together the complex of small settlements that was tied into the center of Hou Ma Chen stretched over more than thirty kilometers. We must imagine that the population numbered in the tens of thousands.

In Hopei Province, near Yi Hsien, a city wall of eight kilometers in length, running from east to west, and four kilometers wide enclosed an area that was internally divided by a great canal. The eastern section of this city was further subdivided into a narrow northern sector containing large dwelling compounds built on raised platforms; the buildings had brick walls, elaborate tile roofs, and eaves and clay drainage pipes. The southern sector contained the dwellings of the workers and the factories. The cemetery was laid out in the northwestern section of the town, but within the garrisoned wall.

In modern Shantung, a town of the state of Ch'i was found near Lin Tzu. A small walled enclosed space lies partially within a larger wall; again the pattern separates a small class of people from the masses of the populace.

The Loyang region of western Honan continued to be a center of Chou activity, and two major cities were built or reoccupied, one during the fifth century and the other towards the end of the third century B.C. The largest, Wang Ch'eng, had walls which enclosed an area of over eight million square meters, but not all the space was in continuous use during the twelve recorded generations. It was divided internally so that workers' quarters and factories were separated by busy thoroughfares from the secluded homes of the nobility. Underground passages lined with tiles drained into the outer moat.

The cemeteries were scattered amongst the suburbs of Loyang and spanned hundreds of years. Some were the burying grounds of the people, small rectangular pits into which the dead were lowered in the flexed position, accompanied by offerings of grain and meat in pottery containers, small utensils of bronze and iron, and jewelry of bone and glass. The lacquered coffins of the wealthy were buried with pomp and riches in underground wooden rooms, the walls painted to simulate hanging carpets and screens. Pottery and bronze figurines were interred as "retainers" to serve the dead; the figurines themselves were bedecked in finery. The pottery figurines were hand-modelled; human beings were shown in postures of action and gesture, while animals frequently had moveable parts—flapping wings, a beak that opened and closed, a head that swivelled on its body.

The people and commodities "of the whole world" came to the noonday markets in these towns. Goods were exchanged in barter, although certain standardized values were placed on cloth and metal coins, and less frequently on chariots and horses. We must also people the market with those merchants and artisans of whom there are no archeological traces—the shoemaker, the food-vendor, the wine merchant, the tailor working on cloth of silk so fine that great lengths when folded could be passed through an earring.

THE CH'U

Iron foundries have been discovered only in the north, in the Yen city of Hsia-tu, in Hopei, but there are clues in the texts and in the composition of the words for iron that its earliest manufacture may have been in Ch'u, or elsewhere in the south. Indeed, the first iron objects to be excavated were from Ch'u tombs.

The iron-tipped plow could dig somewhat more deeply than the stone hoe, but until animal power was harnessed, it did not significantly increase yields. If, however, as Mencius describes the Ch'u, they cleared the fields with fire, then iron axes and sharp-bladed tools made the task of cutting down brush and trees faster, with less expenditure of energy. It was clearly the combination of this ease of clearance and harvesting and the construction of small irrigation works that liberated an entire class of people, permitting them to command the labor of others while creating a courtly life of delicate elegance.

The archeology of Ch'u has barely begun; the histories have not been authenticated, nor the legends collected. Stretching from the Han and Huai river valleys to the central region of many lakes in Hupei and Hunan provinces, along the Hsiang River and the Yangtze itself, the relics of Ch'u bear testament to Ssu Ma Ch'ien's amazement at the vastness and variety. The historian sums up this variety in the classic expression of provincialism: ". . . the men of southern Ch'u are fond of fancy phrases and clever at talking, but what they say can seldom be trusted," and describes the great intermixing of people as they went to and fro over the waterways with cargo of hides, dried fish, lumber, and salt. Only a few of the cities and towns have been recognized archeologically; in part their identification is hindered by continued occupation of the ancient sites. Of these towns, three have earthen walls constructed by the Ch'u; they all enclose roughly rectangular space with contemporary satellite hamlets outside. The walls themselves were impenetrable, one measures twenty-four meters in width and has a "lookout" tower rising five meters at one corner.

There were no rice fields within the towns, although one can imagine that small vegetable gardens were grown. The people in the outlying villages utilized the varied potential of the land, raising their favorite spices and tending orchards of fruit-bearing trees. They supplemented the fish and small animals in their diet with chickens, forever to be intimates of the Chinese household, along with the family pig. Tools were made in local foundries and probably repaired there also. It can be assumed that local markets were created to circulate these items and other goods such as hemp cloth, pottery, bamboo mats and utensils among the farming communities.

An entirely different group of artisans specialized in production for luxury consumption by the townsfolk and for export. The craftsmen of Ch'u were uniquely skilled, achieving heights of workmanship in lacquer ware. Delicately winged-cups, bowls, and screens were painted with beautifully swirling designs, often bringing animal forms and birds into playful opposition to abstracted curvilineal patterns. At other times, realistically drawn court-scenes portray Ch'u women seated in pavilions, wearing long gowns with gracefully draped sleeves, or walking along slowly in small groups, gesturing as they talk. The men, also, are never shown at work, but riding in light chariots or on prancing horses as they chase through the forests, perhaps racing or hunting in sport.

The ceramic workshops produced wheel-made vessels of

fine quality, frequently glazed, and of varied shapes. There were shops that specialized in stone-carving and also places where bamboo was prepared and then fashioned into all manners of containers, bows, musical instruments, and the short sectional slips that were strung together in "books," characters were written on them with brush and ink in the script familiar to that of the Chou, but heavily interspersed with bird designs.

Another genre of art combined elements into symbolic representations that are beyond our grasp. These are wooden images of bird-like, tiger-like creatures, three-headed figures and a pervasive motif of a humanoid head, often with antlers, but always with an elongated, protruding tongue. This art conveys the feeling of something sacred, but not necessarily episodic; it is found in the funerary context of rich tombs. There is little in the material culture or the extant literature of Ch'u to indicate an emphasis on kinship descent through the generations; instead there is a very powerful veneration of nature, and the symbology is one of communication with nature, which transcends time. Perhaps it is the flight of the birds that are so prominent in the art, and the flow of the streams that carry the Ch'u poets on their journeys through many "worlds" that provide temporal continuity and helped to recast diverse ethnic elements into the Ch'u identity.

Here prehistory ends. There is no culmination, no climax. When the great unifying Ch'in emerges from its chrysalis, it spins a web intermeshing the technologies of north and south. A national style of life is gradually formulated, one in which the social relationship to the land changes as peasant and landlord classes are defined, economic relationships are molded in the market place, and politics assume internal and external administrative functions. The Ch'in expansion, and the Han, which followed, was made possible by the multi-focused pattern that was laid a thousand years previous. The south, with its massive irrigation-cultivation, became a major resource of food for the north and raw materials for manufactories everywhere. The bureaucracy that grew out of the administrative needs of the north fostered the literate arts, philosophy, and science.

With this literacy, true historiography begins and archeology serves as its handmaiden, always a corrective but no longer providing a creative reconstruction of the otherwise unknown. The picture painted by the prehistorian is cluttered, but so is everyday.

Suggested Readings

Bibliographies: *Council on Old World Archaeology Survey and Bibliography, Area* 17, 1959, 1961, 1963 Cambridge, Massachusetts.

CHAPTER I

Chang, K. C. "New Evidence on Fossil Man in China, *Science,* 1962, v. 136: 749–60.

Blumenstock, D. ed. *Pleistocene and Post-Pleistocene Climatic Variations in the Pacific Area,* Hawaii, 1966.

Needham, J. *Time and the Eastern Man,* Royal Anthropological Institute of Great Britain and Ireland, Occasional Papers #21, 1965.

Tsukada, M. *Paleogeography, Paleoclimatology, Paleoecology,* 1967 #3: 49–64.

CHAPTER II

Andersson, J. D. "Preliminary Report on Archeological Research in Kansu," *Geological Survey of China,* 1925, ser. A#5.

Chard, C. "Archeology in the Soviet Union," *Science,* 1969, V. 163: 774–779.

Michael, H. N. *The Archeology and Geomorphology of Northern*

Asia, Toronto, 1964 (see articles by Larichev and Okladnikov).

Chêng, T. K. *Archeological Studies in Szechwan*, Cambridge, England, 1957.

Shih, H. P. et al. *Hsi-an Pan P'o*, Peking, 1963.

Waterbolk, H. T. "Food Production in Prehistoric Europe," *Science*, 1969, v. 162: 1093–1101.

CHAPTER III

Chang, K. C. *Archaeology of Ancient China*, rev. 1968, New Haven.

An C. M. et al. *Miao Ti Kuo yu San Li Ch'iao*, Peking, 1959.

Chêng, T. K. *Prehistoric China*, Cambridge, 1959, supplement to above: *New Light on Prehistoric China*, Cambridge, England, 1966.

Treistman, J. M. "Ch'ü Chia Ling" *Asian Perspectives*, 1968, v. XI: 69–91.

CHAPTER IV

Barnard, N. *Bronze Casting and Bronze Alloys in Ancient China*, Tokyo, 1961.

Cheng-ch'ou Ehr-li-kang, Peking, 1959.

Fairbank, W. "Piece mold-casting and Shang bronze design," *Archives of the Chinese Art Society of America*, V. XVI, #9, 1962.

Gettens, R. F. *The Freer Chinese Bronzes*, v. II: Technical Studies, Washington, 1969.

Hansford, S. *Chinese Carved Jades*, Connecticut, 1968.

Shih, C. J. *Yin-hsü Chien-chu Yi-ts'un*, Taipei, 1959.

Umehara, S. *Yin Hsu*, Tokyo, 1964.

CHAPTER V

von Dewall, M. "The Tien Culture of Southwest China," *Antiquity*, 1967, v. 40: 8–21.

Jettmar, K. *Art of the Steppes,* New York, 1967.
Kao, C. H., and Liang, S. Y. *Archaeologica Sinica,* v. III, Taipei, 1962–67.
Li, C. P. *The Chemical Arts of Old China,* Pennsylvania, 1948.
Tung, T. P. *Chia-ku-hsüeh,* Taipei, 1955.
Solheim, W. "Southeast Asia and the West," *Science,* 1967, v. 157: 896–902.
Watson, W. *Ancient Chinese Bronzes,* Vermont, 1962.

CHAPTER VI

Needham, J. *The Development of Iron and Steel Technology in China,* London, 1958.
Chêng, T. K. *Chou China,* Cambridge, 1963.
Shang, H. T. *Ch'ang-sha Ch'u-t'u Ku-tai,* Peking, 1954.

Index